5-23-15

Dear Paul,

As you enter this new stage in your life, my prayer for you is that you will walk "In His light." Ephesians 1:16-19

In Him,
Cherie

In His *Light*

A 60-Day Devotional to Help You
"Walk in the Light as He Is in the Light"
(I John 1:7)

CHERIE HAMMERS

safepasture.org

WESTBOW
PRESS
A DIVISION OF THOMAS NELSON
& ZONDERVAN

Copyright © 2014 Cherie Hammers.

All rights reserved. No part of this book may be used or reproduced by any means, graphic, electronic, or mechanical, including photocopying, recording, taping or by any information storage retrieval system without the written permission of the publisher except in the case of brief quotations embodied in critical articles and reviews.

WestBow Press books may be ordered through booksellers or by contacting:

WestBow Press
A Division of Thomas Nelson & Zondervan
1663 Liberty Drive
Bloomington, IN 47403
www.westbowpress.com
1 (866) 928-1240

Because of the dynamic nature of the Internet, any web addresses or links contained in this book may have changed since publication and may no longer be valid. The views expressed in this work are solely those of the author and do not necessarily reflect the views of the publisher, and the publisher hereby disclaims any responsibility for them.

Any people depicted in stock imagery provided by Bigstock are models, and such images are being used for illustrative purposes only. Certain stock imagery © Bigstock.

ISBN: 978-1-4908-1393-6 (sc)
ISBN: 978-1-4908-1394-3 (hc)
ISBN: 978-1-4908-1392-9 (e)

Library of Congress Control Number: 2013919449

Printed in the United States of America.

WestBow Press rev. date: 3/27/2014

Scriptures taken from the Holy Bible, New International Version®, NIV®. Copyright © 1973, 1978, 1984, 2011 by Biblica, Inc.™ Used by permission of Zondervan. All rights reserved worldwide. www.zondervan.com The "NIV" and "New International Version" are trademarks registered in the United States Patent and Trademark Office by Biblica, Inc.™ All rights reserved.

Scripture taken from the New King James Version. Copyright © 1979, 1980, 1982 by Thomas Nelson, inc. Used by permission. All rights reserved.

Scripture taken from the King James Version of the Bible.

Scripture taken from the Holman Christian Standard Bible ® Copyright © 2003, 2002, 2000, 1999 by Holman Bible Publishers. All rights reserved.

Scripture taken from the Holy Bible: International Standard Version® Release 2.0. Copyright © 1996-2012 by the ISV Foundation. ALL RIGHTS RESERVED INTERNATIONALLY.

Scripture quotations taken from the New American Standard Bible®, Copyright © 1960, 1962, 1963, 1968, 1971, 1972, 1973, 1975, 1977, 1995 by The Lockman Foundation. Used by permission. (www.Lockman.org)

Scripture taken from the *Amplified Bible*, copyright © 1954, 1958, 1962, 1964, 1965, 1987 by The Lockman Foundation. Used by permission.

Scripture taken from the American King James Version of the Bible.

Scripture quotations are from The Holy Bible, English Standard Version® (ESV®), copyright © 2001 by Crossway, a publishing ministry of Good News Publishers. Used by permission. All rights reserved.

Scripture quotations taken from the Holy Bible, New Living Translation, Copyright © 1996, 2004. Used by permission of Tyndale House Publishers, Inc., Wheaton, Illinois 60189. All rights reserved.

Contents

Foreword xi
Introduction xiii
Dedication xv

Give a Mouse a Cookie 1
The Victory Storehouse 5
Do Not Conform 7
Living Sacrifices 11
Shedding 15
Eternity 19
Flooded with Hope 23
Can You Hear Me Now? 25
Strongholds 29
Faith & Unbelief 33
Free As the Deer 37
Justice, Mercy, and Humility 39
Give and It Shall Be Given Unto You 43
Perfect Peace 47
Quack 49
He that Dwelleth 53

Dwelling in the Shelter 55
Under the Shadow 57
I Will Say of the Lord 59
Snare of the Fowler 63
The Truth of God. 65
Lessons from an Elephant 67
If God Be For Us 69
The Chicken and the Banana Peel 71
Above All Else Guard Your Heart. 75
The Worth of a Donkey. 77
The God of the Impossible. 79
Faith and Grace 81
Disappointment 85
Singing in the Rain 87
Healing & Worship 89
Broken Pieces. 93
Looking unto Jesus. 95
The Oven Door 97
Jesus Talked to a Tree. 101
The Fig Tree Died 103
Your Negative Situation Needs Attention 105
Cursing the Fig Tree 109
Caterpillar to Butterfly. 111

Restored	113
Parasites	115
Little Bitty Batter	117
What Do You Think?	119
He Holds Victory in Store	121
Camouflage	125
Ephesians 5 & You	127
Building on the Rock	129
Speak to Your Mountain	133
Just Ducky	135
The GPS Mess	137
Squirrely Thieves	139
Prodigals & Pigs	143
A Farmer Went Out to Sow	147
The Dirty Window	151
Believing God	155
Worthless Pursuits	157
Courageous Sheep	161
Freedom	163
Fruitless Trees	165
What's That Smell?	167
Receiving Jesus as Your Savior	171
About the Author	173

Foreword

Within a short period of time after meeting Cherie, I could see that she had a great desire to share the Gospel with anyone and everyone she could. She consistently had a testimony about people to whom she had witnessed or ministered. One thing I noticed was the way she answered the questions of those with whom she was sharing. The Holy Spirit would give Cherie a unique perspective to help that individual and I would think, "That's really good!" I see the same application throughout this devotional, "In His Light". Every chapter is built upon a sound foundation of Scripture. Like an interior decorator, she has a graceful way of presenting the Word in an attractive manner. I believe this devotional will be a blessing to those who read it.

Pastor Bill Adcock,
Word & Spirit Church

Introduction

How many times in your life have you seen something happen that taught you a Biblical lesson? Have you ever had an experience that gave you the idea God was tapping you on the shoulder and pointing at something in your life? I have had many such happenings and have written them down in my journal to record what God was revealing to me. I realized that others might benefit from these insights, which resulted in the birth of this book. My hope is that walking through this collection of essays will be a pilgrimage you will not soon forget. Throughout this journey, my desire is that you will internalize His love and will shine like the stars "*in His Light*".

Dedication

To my Heavenly Father

all glory, praise and honor

And to my family

whose love and support

brought this desire of my

heart into reality

Give a Mouse a Cookie

> Catch for us the foxes, the little foxes that ruin the vineyards, our vineyards that are in bloom.
>
> Song of Solomon 2:15, NIV

• • • • • • •

There it was again. The sound of a tiny army marching across the exposed pipes in my college trailer bedroom. It seemed it was only a week ago when my roommate and I discovered a rather plump mouse running around the living room furniture. We had done a lot of screaming and looking, but that was the extent of it. Now we realized that the "plump" mouse had really been in the family way and we were not really sure how many occupants were in our trailer.

Even though they were small in size, this army of mice had become my focus. Okay, the word *obsession* would be more appropriate. When I went to class, I wondered how we were going to solve this problem. When I came home for lunch, I pondered it. When I went to bed, I worried about where these mice went at night since I knew they were nocturnal. In short, I was becoming paranoid. And with good reason.

One day I came home for lunch and proceeded to fix myself a ham sandwich. As I stood there in the middle of the kitchen floor, I had the unsettling feeling that I was being watched. I looked to the left and then to the right. For some strange reason, I looked down. There between my feet, was a mouse all of one and a half inches long looking up at me. I screamed, he squeaked, and ham, lettuce, and bread went airborne!

Nighttime was much worse. I would fall asleep to the tinkling sound of untold numbers of mice feet marching on the water pipes near the head of my bed. My dreams were full of these mice. Once I thought I was dreaming about hearing the sound of mouse feet scrunching across my mattress. I thought, *This is only a dream. Mice aren't in my bed. How silly!* I continued to have this discussion with myself in my head until it was interrupted by a real-life cold mouse nose touching my real-life arm!

The moral of this story? Focus on eradicating the one mouse before it becomes six mice! How often does a little sin scurry across the living room of our hearts and we are a little unsettled, but we tell ourselves, "That's really not a big deal. Especially when I think about So-and-So and his issues. Now if I had *his* issues, I would be doing something." All the while, our "little" problems are multiplying and becoming more and more entrenched in our hearts. The "little" issue has not only caused damage in the living room of our hearts, it now has run of the whole house. Now it has gotten our attention because there is no ignoring it. Now we have become obsessed because it dogs our every step and steals our joy. We have become entangled in "the sin which doth so easily beset us," (Hebrews 12:1, KJV).

But don't worry. God is our deliverer. He can get us out of this mess. It will take repentance and submission on our part and it will be painful. But He can get our lives back on track according to His will. The sad fact is we have not eradicated this sin at the outset which means we will waste so much more time and energy;

and our lives will be unnecessarily tormented. God wants us free to do His will, not chasing a litter of mice around the house or staying awake at night wondering how to do damage control. Jesus said in John 10:10, "The thief comes not, but to steal, and to kill, and to destroy. I have come that they might have life and that they might have it more abundantly," (NKJV).

One major facet of this abundant life is to be a builder in the kingdom. But you can't be an effective kingdom builder if you are allowing sin to draw you into "confusion and every evil work," (James 3:16, KJV). Satan has set a trap for you. So set a few traps of your own. And live in the freedom Jesus purchased for you.

The Victory Storehouse

> He holds victory in store for the upright.
>
> Proverbs 2:7, NIV

During my prayer walk this morning, the Lord brought to my mind the above Scripture. God impressed upon me this thought, "I have a storehouse. Remember, I talked about it in the book of Job. I have thunderbolts, snow, hail, etc. But I have victory in store for you." Then I thought about another Scripture verse that says, "This is the victory that overcomes the world, even our faith," I John 5:4 (NKJV).

Faith is how we get into the storehouse. Faith gives us the access and opens the door. Another Scripture tells us, "Faith comes by hearing and hearing by the Word of God," Romans 10:17 (NKJV). So, when we get the Word into our hearts, we get the keys to the storehouse of blessing that God has put aside for us. God has given us an inheritance through Jesus' payment on the cross.

Hebrews 11:1, says, "Faith is the substance of things hoped for, the evidence of things not seen," (KJV). We cannot see the storehouse with our natural eyes. But, as we read the Word, we can see with our spiritual eyes, the eyes of faith, the abundance of blessing that

God has so graciously provided for us. There is *substance* to what we are believing God for. It is as real as the nose on your face! We just need the bridge of faith to be able to bring it from the spiritual realm into the physical realm. Paul said we need to "focus not on what is seen, but on what is unseen," 2 Cor. 4:18 (HCSB). When we look at what is unseen, we are looking with the eyes of faith. Soon what is unseen will be seen!

Romans 8:6 tells us that "to be carnally-minded is death, but to be spiritually-minded is life and peace," (KJV). To have victory in life brings a sense of peace. For example, if you owe a huge bill and the company you owe is breathing down your neck, this situation has the potential to be a stressful one. If you choose to be carnally minded, that is, focused on your natural circumstances, you will be envisioning things like bill collectors calling you, not being able to pay your other bills, or your finances tanking--the death of your dreams and happiness. On the other hand, if you turn your attention to spiritual things, such as prayer, claiming God's promises, reading the Word, and trusting God, you will have a sense of peace that God is taking care of your life.

So grab the key of your faith and take a stroll to the warehouse. Your Father and your victory are waiting for you.

Do Not Conform

> Do not conform any longer to the pattern of this world . . .
>
> Romans 12:2, NIV

Have you ever been to an 1800's era historic site and seen some of the tools and utensils the people back then used in daily life? These items are very interesting to say the least, and I am always impressed with their ingenuity. One thing that I never get tired of seeing is the butter molds. They were not necessary in the making of butter, but each family had a design unique to that family. They were decorative and creative. I've seen several versions of the butter molds, and every time I see one, I am reminded of the above text.

You see, our minds are similar to soft butter. Not to be offensive, but we are so easily influenced by our environment. Look at our culture and the impressions it is making on our society. The pattern of this world is going against God and everything He stands for. The Bible tells us not to be ignorant of the Devil and his devices. Satan is sly and subtle. He will bring philosophies that have an element of truth to them and then attach subtle deception to them. The Bible says that through these philosophies, the Devil traps people to do his will.

That sounds pretty scary, doesn't it? What are we to do? I mean, we are constantly being pressed from every side by our environment. Little do we realize that not only are we being conformed to the world, but our hearts are being hardened in the process as well. God has the antidote for our dilemma. Not only does He tell us what *not* to do, "Do not conform any longer to the pattern of this world" (Romans 12:2a), He tells us what we *should* do. Through the apostle Paul, He says, "But be transformed by the renewing of your mind," (Romans 12:2b).

When you renew your mind to the Word of God, it affords you protection around both your heart and mind. Let's say you have just applied for the job of your dreams. First Peter 5:7 reads, "Casting all your care upon Him, because He cares for you," (NKJV). You begin to meditate on this verse until you have God's peace about the situation. Then Satan comes to you with the thought, *I'm probably not going to get this job. Oh no! What am I going to do?* You reach back in your mental files, pull out 1 Peter 5:7, and answer that doubt with "I resist you, Satan. I have already cast the care of this situation onto the Lord. So if you want to talk to somebody about this, go talk to Jesus because He is the one who is in charge of who gets this job." Immediately, your peace will return to you and the fear will leave. Truly, being forewarned is being forearmed.

Not being conformed to this world and instead being transformed by the renewing of your mind is likened to concrete. When it is first poured, it can easily conform to the shape of the mold into which it is poured. I ask you, of what use would concrete be if it never set up? It would be useless. Try walking on a sidewalk that never became rock-hard. How would this work for you, especially if you were wearing high heels? No, that would never do. The concrete would constantly be in a state of being conformed. Once you took the mold boards away, the concrete would ooze away.

Transformation is what this concrete would need. It would need to be transformed from something whose form could easily change to a substance that is rock-hard when dry.

God desires this for our minds. He wants us to be solid in His truth so that we will not be easily pressured by the world to conform to its standards, and be "blown about by every wind of doctrine," (Ephesians 4:14, ISV).

Another important benefit of filling our minds with the Word is in Romans 12:2, "Then you will be able to test and approve what God's will is—His good, pleasing and perfect will." When you know God's Word, you will get guidance on decisions you make every day. You will know the character of God and will sense His peace when you follow the Word you have been meditating on.

So, conform your mind to be rock-solid on God's Word. Oh, and could you please pass the butter?

Living Sacrifices

> Offer your bodies as a living sacrifice, holy and pleasing to God . . .
>
> Romans 12:1 NIV

Yesterday, we talked about the importance of keeping our minds renewed to the Word of God. It is interesting to note that the apostle Paul has in no way made a friendly suggestion to us. Rather, he is commanding us not conform to the pattern of the world.

Now, before we start making excuses for ourselves, copping out and saying that there is no way we can do this, that it is humanly impossible to guard what we say in stressful situations, let's back up a verse. And let's put in perspective the mandate God has given us pertaining to renewing our minds. Romans 12:1 says, "Therefore, I urge you, brothers, in view of God's mercy, to offer your bodies as living sacrifices, holy and pleasing to God—this is your spiritual act of worship."

Because of God's great mercy to us in redeeming us from the wages of our sin, we owe God our very lives. We are to offer our bodies as living sacrifices. When we take charge of our bodies to make them walk in God's will for our lives, we will be holy (set apart) and pleasing to God.

What do you use to direct your body in the right direction? Right! Your mind. If your mind is not thinking thoughts after God and His ways, your body will not be able to obey God. Your mind is the decision-maker for your body. For instance, let's say you are sitting on the couch watching your favorite television show. You suddenly remember you forgot to do your daily Bible reading.

Your mind now has a decision to make: do you stay where you are, or do turn off the set and get your Bible? Who is in charge? If your mind chose to keep you where you were, your body would not be able to move to get the Bible. It would sit there until your mind gave it another instruction.

Getting back to our opening verse, would turning off the television qualify as a sacrifice? Of course it would. You would be sacrificing something you wanted to do for something God wanted you to do. Would your obedience qualify as holy?

Yes, setting yourself apart for God's service is holy. Would reading your Bible in place of television be considered pleasing to God? Again, yes. Our obedience, as fragrant incense, comes up before the Lord as a pleasing aroma. Also, when the Lord drops into our hearts to do something, there is always a reason, even if it is not always apparent to us at the time.

Let's don't forget the end of verse 1. God says that when we have offered our bodies as living sacrifices, this is our spiritual act of worship. Going back to our earlier scenario, is God saying that getting up off the couch, turning off the TV, and grabbing the Bible is equivalent to worshipping Him? Yes! How can that be, you may ask?

First of all, a cursory look at the word *worship* will reveal a big clue. This word literally means, "worth-ship". When you worship God, you are, in essence, telling God that He is worthy of adoration. Likewise, when you obey God, especially in the presence of temptation, you are telling God that He is worthy of your service, that He is worth getting what He wants (you reading the Bible) over your flesh getting what it wants (watching television).

One small reminder. We are living sacrifices. Living sacrifices have a nasty habit of getting up and crawling off the altar. Your flesh is always present with you, wanting to get its way. You must, through the renewing of your mind, keep your flesh under subjection. Keep it on the altar as a living sacrifice that is holy and pleasing to God.

Shedding

> The love of God is shed abroad in our hearts by the Holy Spirit who is given unto us.
>
> Romans 5:5, NKJV

I was taking my morning walk during which I some have quiet time with the Lord. I prayed that God would take my day and use it the way He desired. Happily, I had remembered to give Him the day, as many a day I have asked for His blessing, but not His schedule. Anyway, I had not even walked ten minutes before the young man who lived at the end of the street had turned down our road. His family had moved there about a year previously, but I had only spoken to him once before. As my walk was about to take me across his driveway, I stopped to let him pass. To my surprise, he rolled down the window and chatted about what a pleasant day it was. I asked if he were a college student. He said he was, so I inquired of him as to his major and also found out that he would be graduating next month. I congratulated him on his achievement and wished him a pleasant weekend.

As I continued on my walk, and once again turned my thoughts back to God, I thanked Him for the opportunity to speak with this young man who was obviously pleased with the interest I had taken in him. My goal is to have more small conversations that lead to encouraging him in the Lord. I prayed for his salvation as I talked with the Lord, and I felt a surge of joy over this encounter. The Lord then reminded me of Romans 5:5, "The love of God has been shed abroad in our hearts," (NKJV). I heard the Lord speak to my heart, "I have given you My love to give to others. That is where the joy comes from."

I began to meditate on that word "shed". What is my experience with shedding? Why, of course! Our cats! Have you ever held a cat and put it down without having it shed some fur on you? Every close encounter you have with a cat leaves a trace. That cat has imparted something to you. (Now I'm not talking about those encounters that involve claws or teeth, because the cat does impart something more painful in those situations.)

I have a Siamese cat that has creamy white fur. I like to wear a couple of T-shirts that are dark blue. So when I pick her up and later find myself in front of a mirror, I am always amazed at how many cat hairs she has left behind. You would think if I picked her up a few more times, she should be completely bald! But she's not. There is always more where that came from!

So it is with the love of God. When we interact with people, when we minister to them, even if it is just a kind word or smile, we are shedding the love of God to others. God's love is sticking to their hearts and they may be unable to put their finger on just what is happening. But God's Word also tells us that "God's kindness leads you toward repentance," (Romans 2:4, NIV). What you are shedding on someone's heart, God is using to lead that person to Himself.

The next time you want to shy away from starting up a conversation with that person in line in front of you at the grocery store, just think about how a cat rubs on a person's leg. Just go shed some of God's love on that person, and feel the joy of the Lord well up inside of you. You just might find yourself purring.

Eternity

> God has put eternity in men's hearts . . .
>
> Ecclesiastes 3:11, NKJV

I grew up in a farming community where most of our neighbors were relatives. I had a sweet, hard-working great-aunt who lived about a half mile down our little country road. I have fond memories of pedaling my bicycle with the banana seat along that grassy-middle country lane. Aunt Carrie lived in an old country farmhouse. As soon as she spotted us atop her hilly driveway, she could be seen welcoming us into her charming little kitchen. Once we were seated around her tiny dining table, Aunt Carrie would open the door to a small white pantry housing a candy dish which always offered some delightful treat.

And my aunt was always truly interested in what my siblings and I were doing, and what we were into. Later she still seemed genuinely sad to see us go. It never occurred to me as a child that when we dropped in to see her unannounced, we were actually interrupting her day. Because of her lovely heart and gracious demeanor, we always felt like the guests of honor in her house.

I looked upon visits to her house with great anticipation due to the kindness of her gentle heart. It was a peaceful haven to come to rest, eat candy, and visit for a spell. Sometimes we would walk around her small front yard that she or Uncle Harry still mowed with an old-fashioned reel lawn mower. The back yard really didn't need mowing because of the chickens that resided there. Even as a young child I remember walking alongside the house in the area connecting these two yards and looking out beyond the back yard into the fields that seemed to never end. There were times I would behold those fields during a hazy summer evening, and was convinced I was looking at the borders of heaven. I would stand there gazing at that beauty, contemplating what life in heaven must be like. I had eternity set in my heart.

Every human being has eternity placed in his heart. Every person knows that he was made to worship something or someone. There have been native tribes found in various parts of the world that have existed for centuries closed off from the rest of civilization. Yet each one, without exception, has worshipped some entity. We are spiritual creatures. Because we are creatures, we know instinctively that there is someone higher we answer to. And because we are spiritual, we will worship *something*.

Eternity is a word of which we have limited the meaning. When most people think of the word *eternity*, they think of heaven. Some may even think of hell as well. But most people think of eternity as being *something that happens after you die*. I learned recently that Jesus actually gave us a different definition of the word *eternity*.

John 17:3 says, "This is eternal life, that they may know You, the only true God, and Jesus Christ whom You have sent," (NASB). So eternity is to *know* who God is. It is to know Him intimately and to have a thriving relationship with Him. Solomon said that God has put eternity in our hearts. The desire to know God is in every person. Every human spirit craves an intimate *knowing* of their Creator.

When can we have eternity? As soon as we can begin having relationship with God. And that begins the moment we invite Jesus into our hearts, repent of our sins, and ask for forgiveness. We were meant to have eternity now.

We can enjoy our thoughts of heaven, too. Just don't forget about the eternity that is *now*.

Flooded with Hope

> Now the God of hope fill you with all joy and peace in believing, that you may abound in hope, through the power of the Holy Spirit.
>
> Romans 15:13, NKJV

I was talking with my Aunt Mary recently telling her about how our donkey broke a pipe beneath the pump out beside our chicken house. By the time we found the leak, there was a moat around the coop and the chickens were enjoying the cool fresh, bubbling water.

Aunt Mary in turn relayed the story of the flood that happened in her town in 1957. She said that they had a litter of nine boxer puppies and had sold all but one and the mother. When the flood happened, she and my uncle had two feet of water in the basement. They scrambled to get a sump pump downstairs and when they got that situation under control, they rushed out to the backyard to check on the dogs. What they found was the puppy and its mother on the roof of the doghouse. It seemed that they were waiting for the next boat to come by!

What struck me about these dogs was that they were full of hope. Although the water kept rising, possibly for hours, these boxers did what was within their power. They climbed to the top of their doghouse and waited to be rescued. That, I believe, is what God wants our response to be to the trials we face. When the flood waters come rushing into our lives, threatening to destroy everything we have, do we panic or calmly do what we can, leaving the rest to God? In Romans 15:13 it says, "May the God of hope fill you with joy and peace as you trust in Him so that you may overflow with hope by the power of the Holy Spirit," (NIV).

When floods of trials come into our lives, God wants to flood our lives with joy and peace. But we must avail ourselves of God's power through our trust in Him. Then we will overflow, or be flooded, with hope by the power of the Holy Spirit. We will see His power manifest in our lives in a way we could not have had otherwise. And we certainly would not have seen these supernatural results had we flipped out, thinking that God would not come through for us.

So the next time you hear the rain coming, look at your dog and see if he seems to be in a panic. Chances are he is flooded with hope.

Can You Hear Me Now?

> If I regard iniquity in my heart, the Lord will not hear me.
>
> Psalm 66:18, NKJV

How many times have you been in a remote or a not-so-remote area and your cell phone will not get a signal. It's very frustrating. At times like that I have a fantasy of throwing my cell phone like a baseball pitcher throws a ball across home plate. I have joked before that my cell phone seems to be one step up from 2 cans and a string! There are times in my house when all I have to do is simply walk into another room while I'm on the phone and I lose the signal. I've tried holding the phone up to the ceiling while standing on one foot. It doesn't seem to work too well. Maybe I need to be wearing a tin foil hat.

Sometimes our communication with God seems to be along the same track. The signal doesn't seem to be too clear so we think that maybe a "method" will help; some 1-2-3 solution to get God to speak to us. Maybe if we just pray more, get involved in more programs at church, or get into one more Bible study, God will speak to us more clearly. So we go full steam ahead, trying to make our new system work. But soon we find ourselves not really hearing anything more and feeling very weary. Why can't we get a clear signal from God?

Well, as the old saying goes, when all else fails, read the instructions. When you feel as if God is not speaking to you, go back to His instruction manual, the Bible. The Scripture says, "Draw near to God and He will draw near to you," (James 4:8, NKJV) How do you draw near to God? First of all, you must deal with any sin in your life. In Psalm 66:18 it says "If I regard iniquity in my heart, the Lord will not hear me," (NKJV). If I have sin in my heart, God has withdrawn Himself. He will not dwell in the presence of sin. If you could picture this, sin is standing between you and God. It is blocking your communication. Repentance gets that sin out of the way. Repentance is drawing near to God. God's ear is bent toward a repentant heart. Isaiah 42:3 says "A bruised reed He will not break and a smoking wick He will not snuff out," (NIV). When you are broken over your sin, God doesn't condemn you. He puts His arm around you!

But maybe you are not in open sin. Maybe you seem to be doing everything right, but still your relationship with God doesn't seem to be where it needs to be. Look at your priorities. How are you spending your time? Does God take first place? Is He truly your Master? Or is He just a convenient troubleshooter that helps you out in your time of need, your tech support?

One of the Beatitudes states, "Blessed are the pure in heart for they shall see God," (Matthew 5:8, NASB). When your heart is pure there is nothing hindering God from manifesting Himself to you and through you. However, impurity repels the Holy Spirit. God said, "Be holy because I am holy," 1 Peter 1:16 (NIV). It's time to take a good hard look at your media intake. What books, movies, television shows, and internet sites are you taking in? "Aw," you say, "I watch that stuff and I know it has some questionable scenes in it. But it doesn't affect me. I'm not going to do those things. I just enjoy it for the entertainment."

I ask you, would you feel any differently about that *questionable* TV show if Jesus were physically sitting with you on the couch? Secondly, is that program or You Tube video worth sacrificing your intimacy with God? Is your relationship with God really worth that movie because you deserve some entertainment?

Here is another consideration about your communication problem. Are you spending time listening for God's voice? I've heard people say, "I just can't understand what God's will is." But as I converse with them further, I find out that quiet time with God is not a top priority. I would say that if I didn't turn on a radio, tune it in, and then listen to it, I wouldn't know what was being said over those airwaves. It's not that those radio announcers are not speaking. The problem is that I'm not tuned in and listening. Likewise, if I don't tune in to receive God's "signals" I will not know what He is saying to me. Romans 12:2 explains that if we want to know God's will, we will be required to renew our minds to His Word. God's direction will be become clear to us as we spend time with Him.

So you can put your foot down, rest your arm, and get the tinfoil off your head. God wants to speak to you more than you want to hear from Him. Can you hear Him now?

Strongholds

> For though we walk in the flesh, we do not war after the flesh. For the weapons of our warfare are not carnal, but mighty through God to the pulling down of strongholds, casting down imaginations and every high thing that exalts itself against the knowledge of God, and bringing into captivity every thought unto the obedience of Christ.
>
> 2 Corinthians 10:3-5, NKJV

Strongholds are walls that provide protection, especially in a time of war. Let's face it. We are at war with demonic forces and they are looking for a place of protection. One day in church our pastor was talking about how in the Greek, the phrase *pulling down* means *to completely destroy to the point that it cannot be put back together again*. In other words, there is not even rubble that is recognizable. That is how thoroughly God destroys strongholds.

Through a series of revelations, I had begun to realize that this digestive problem I have had for years was indeed a stronghold. The weapons God gave me were meant to completely annihilate this stronghold, but after reading the verse carefully, I saw that

God doesn't pull them down; *I* am supposed to be using these very weapons to destroy them.

One day, while in prayer, I asked the Lord, "Okay, if this is something You designed for me to do, how do I do this? I need to know a 1-2-3 method or something." He simply responded, "Read the rest of that verse." I did.

Here was my 1-2-3 method:

1. Cast down imaginations.
2. Cast down every high thing that exalts itself against the knowledge of God.
3. Bring into captivity every thought unto the obedience of Christ.

Cast down imaginations. When you have had a health problem for quite some time, you begin to have an *image* on the inside of you of how life is going to be from now on. Satan will tell you this is never going to get better, or maybe you are going to die from it. He is painting images in your mind. He has impressed your mind with the idea that your new identity is a sick person. When he throws those images up on the screen of your mind, you need to cast them down. Don't toy with those thoughts. As soon as you recognize them for what they are, put these lies under your feet.

Cast down every high thing that exalts itself against the knowledge of God. When you have a thought that is not in line with God's Word, that thought is exalting itself against the knowledge of God. When your sickness is telling you that it is never going to leave, that it will overcome your health, that you will never recover, this negative thought has told you that it is more powerful than anything else in your life, including God. Sickness has declared itself a high thing and is exalting itself. That thing needs to be cast down. When this lie is talking to you, don't entertain it. Cast it down and begin to talk to *it* about God and *His* Power.

Bring every thought captive unto the obedience of Christ. Every thought that you have concerning this situation has to submit to the will of God. If a particular thought doesn't line up with the Word of God, then it is a disobedient thought and needs to be arrested by God's Word.

Something God showed me about a stronghold is that it is built brick by brick. These bricks are basically thoughts that have been presented to you and you have received them. For instance, you have a pain in your back, and the thought comes to you, *My back hurts.* Your mind gives its consent and your thoughts move forward, *I wonder how I hurt my back. I wonder if my back will hurt tomorrow? Maybe I should call in sick tomorrow,* and on and on it goes. Brick by brick the wall gets built. Let me tell you what is behind that wall.

Jesus said that when a spirit goes out of a man, it goes through arid places seeking a place to dwell. It will then go back to that man from whom it came, and find its former home swept clean, and put in order. It then goes out and brings back seven spirits more wicked than itself. There is something in this man's heart that provided the wall for the stronghold. The spirit was driven out from behind that wall. It began to look for another place to live and decided to go back to see if that particular stronghold was still standing. Finding its former residence not only still existing, but actually clean and put in order, the spirit decided to move back in and bring along roommates.

So it is imperative that you should cast out the demon, but you must tear down the stronghold as well. In other words, you must cast out the demonic force, and then begin to dismantle the stronghold of thoughts behind which that demon force was able to hide.

Don't provide the Devil and his comrades with free real estate. Evict them, tear down the stronghold, and begin breaking ground for the stronghold of the Lord.

Faith & Unbelief

> Abraham did not waver through unbelief, but was strengthened in his faith and gave glory to God, being fully persuaded that God had power to do what He had promised.
>
> Romans 4:20-21 NIV

I've been listening to some teaching recently about how faith and unbelief work. When Jesus had come down from the mountain and the man with the son possessed by an evil spirit asked Him to help, Jesus asked for the boy to be brought to Him. He then prayed, and the boy was delivered immediately of the evil spirit from which he was suffering. The disciples came and asked Jesus why they were unable to drive out the evil spirit. Jesus replied, "This kind can come out only by prayer and fasting," (Mark 9:29, ISV).

Now, I have heard on more than one occasion people explaining that this passage is about Jesus instructing the disciples that there are different ways to deal with various demonic spirits. But what Jesus was referring to when He said, "This kind," was the spirit of unbelief.

This particular spirit is put into force when our five senses speak against what the Bible says is true. Look at what happened in this story. The disciples had obviously prayed for this young man and tried to drive the evil spirit from him. Then their eyes looked at the boy and what they saw told them that their prayer of faith had not worked. Unbelief was speaking to them. Unbelief, which used the five senses to war against faith, won the victory.

Jesus, on the other hand, was not moved by what He saw. He was only moved by faith. Why wasn't His faith defeated by unbelief? That's the question the disciples were really asking. And He gave them an answer. He said, "This kind comes out only by prayer and fasting." So what does that mean? First we have to understand how fasting really works.

Fasting, or going without food for a period of time, is not something a person does to *make* God do something, to twist His arm, so to speak. Rather, fasting is a spiritual discipline that trains your body to submit to your spirit. When you start a fast, your body will begin to rebel against you. It will tell you that you cannot go on without food, that you need to quit now, that you cannot finish this fast. You need to tell your body *no* and go on with your time of prayer. As you continue this discipline, eventually your body will submit to your spirit and quiet down. In essence, your body will back down as your spirit becomes stronger in faith.

Jesus had obviously been practicing this spiritual discipline because, not only did His faith come out the winner, but He knew what had made His faith strong when He was questioned about it. How many nights had He spent praying to the Father? He had flesh to contend with just like you and me. During His intimate time of prayer with His Father, He had consistently put His flesh under submission. He had to train His body to obey the faith of His spirit.

I was meditating on these things one morning in my prayer time and I was wondering how this works. The Holy Spirit brought this thought to my heart: Faith comes by hearing and hearing by the Word of God, (Romans 10:17, NKJV). Unbelief goes away by prayer and fasting. That's it! Faith is to your spirit as exercise is to your muscles. The more you exercise your faith, the stronger it becomes. Unbelief on the other hand, affects your five senses, your flesh nature. When prayer and fasting is applied to the flesh nature, unbelief, like an unused muscle, begins to atrophy. And just like a muscle, it is ever-present and ready for the opportunity to be strengthened again.

So faith affects the strength of your spirit nature and unbelief affects the strength of your flesh nature. You get to choose. It is up to you. You get to decide, by your actions and spiritual disciplines, who will win the battle.

Free As the Deer

For You LORD, will bless the uncompromisingly righteous; as with a shield You will surround him with goodwill (pleasure and favor).

Psalm 5:12, Amp

The thief comes only in order to steal and kill and destroy. I came that they may have and enjoy life, and have it in abundance (to the full, till it overflows).

John 10:10, Amp

As I was turning down our long driveway one night, the sweeping headlights caught the forms of four deer in the neighbor's yard. It was a clear, starlit night, and these deer were not merely grazing. They were *playing. Frolicking. Dancing.* Call it what you like, but these animals obviously did not have a care in the world.

I pondered this scene. If a timid, skittish creature such as a deer can spend time away from the constant vigil of survival, why can't I? I mean, it was dark and predators could have been lurking everywhere. There was grass all around. Why weren't they eating while food was plentiful? Playing seems like such an impractical thing to do, yet they were engaged in a lively game of Chase.

A possible answer to this apparent contradiction is this: God did not create us simply to *survive* this life. Yes, Jesus knew that we would have troubles in this world. He knew that we should be ever vigilant against our enemy who prowls around like a roaring lion. Yet, He comforts us with the knowledge that He has overcome this troubling world. He said He came to give us life and life abundantly.

So why do we not throw our cares on Him and have a time of refreshing play? Because we do not really believe He is telling us the truth. We think we are the only show in town. If we don't look out for ourselves, then who will? If we truly believed God and took Him at His Word, we would be anxious for nothing. We would allow joy and peace to rule in our hearts. In fact, *rejoice* literally means to "spin around with joy". Paul says, "Rejoice in the Lord always and again I say, 'Rejoice,'" (Philippians 4:4, NKJV).

Yes, we need to take care of the necessities over which God has given us stewardship. But sometimes, when we begin to count our blessings and think about the goodness of God, we need to go out in the yard and spin around. Take the time to rejoice!

Justice, Mercy, and Humility

> To act justly, to love mercy, and to walk humbly with your God.
>
> Micah 6:8, NIV

As I was meditating upon this verse, the Lord began to unfold to me some of the manifold gold nuggets contained therein. First of all, *to act justly*. Why, with all the talk of mercy throughout the Bible, would God tell us to seek justice? For one thing, God is a God of order. Without a system of law, the quality of life in our world would be complete and utter chaos.

Many times in the Old Testament, it was said of Israel that there was no law in the land—everyone did as they saw fit. Times like these are dangerous. It means people can steal, commit adultery, or even kill with no penalty and no recourse for the victim. As a result, people live in fear. There is a spirit of distrust and negativity. Justice, however, shuts down the evildoer, restores freedom, and brings back peace and well-being. True justice is not delivered in the spirit of oppression, which seeks to rule with an iron fist, but with a spirit of fairness that desires the best for all involved. Justice is based on a system of laws that sets the standard by which people are to live.

Secondly, *love mercy*. Today, in our society, talk of mercy seems to be everywhere. Criminals get out of prison early, based on "mercy", while victims seem to be disregarded. Is this true mercy? Mercy is based on justice. If a victim's loss is ignored, then justice has not been in place. And if justice has not been in place, then mercy has not been present either. Actually, the perpetrator has gotten away with his crime. For someone to be granted mercy, justice would have already been brought to bear. Justice metes out the punishment; mercy reduces or eliminates that punishment. Justice gives the evildoer what he *deserves*. Mercy gives the evildoer what he does *not* deserve.

I heard an illustration which seems to make this idea more applicable. Suppose you were the accused brought into court to determine the punishment for your collection of parking tickets. If the judge said, "For your crime, you will have to pay a $100 fine," that would be justice. You got what your crime deserved. But also suppose that you told the judge that you were truly sorry, that you would not do it again, and to please forgive the fine because you had just lost your job. And the judge said, "I will cancel your fine." That is mercy. You were brought to justice, but you did not get what you deserved.

God wants us to act justly and love mercy. These are characteristics of God's nature. But God also added, "Walk humbly with your God." How does this pertain to these already balanced areas of how to relate to others? God wants us to relate to Him with humility in order to keep justice and mercy in check.

If one walks humbly with God in the area of justice, then the authority of meting out justice will not go to his head and turn him into a despot. If one walks humbly with God in the area of mercy, then his head will not be turned by bribery. If we do not walk humbly with God, then justice and mercy will soon be turned into cheap counterfeits. Not keeping these three in balance will lead into wickedness and corruption, not just for those directly involved in the justice system, but in our personal lives as well.

Keeping justice, mercy, and humility in balance lead to a life of simplicity, blessing, and peace.

It is a balancing act. But it is worth it.

Give and It Shall Be Given Unto You

> Give and it shall be given unto you; a good measure, pressed down, and shaken together, and running over, shall men give into your bosom.
>
> Luke 6:38, KJV

Today I find myself struggling to trust God for finances. We had some unexpected expenses that just seemed to pile up as the month has gone on. I've heard it said if you have a need, plant a seed. So I opened up my heart to the direction of the Spirit of God, especially in the area of giving finances. I have given more this month than I have in a long time, but my logical mind, aided by the spirit of fear, has reasoned, "You have less money to pay bills because you gave more. It makes perfect sense."

But I, like David in Psalm 91, must take charge of my will, which decides what my mind shall think and dwell on. I might not be in danger from an enemy army like David was, but the threat of my adversary is just as real. So I must declare to myself, *I will say of the LORD, "He is my refuge, and my fortress: my God; in Him will I trust,"* (Psalm 91:2, NKJV).

When I think about my financial situation, I must stop the worry, and declare that God is my refuge; He will shelter me. He is a wall to protect me from destruction; He will keep my enemies at bay. They will not have access to me. He is my God; He is the one I worship, therefore I am submitted to Him and dependant on Him to take care of me. I will trust in Him. I am throwing myself completely on His grace and am totally vulnerable.

Now that I have this settled, I can move on to trusting the promise of God. He said if I gave, it would be given to me. He will move on the hearts of people to give to me. That part is a barrier I have trouble overcoming. I can believe for God to supernaturally touch my body for healing, or to give me direction by His Spirit when I am confused. But I balk when it comes to believing that *people* will be moved by His Spirit. It is so easy to see the faults and even wickedness of those around us and think, "How is God going to move on people? They need money, too! Why would they give to me?"

In doing this, I am discrediting God by my unbelief, which the Bible says is a sin. I must remind my feeble faith that God owns the cattle on a thousand hills. The earth is the Lord's and the fullness therein. God owns everything and He can get it to me by any means necessary. He said in Deuteronomy 28 that I am the head and not the tail, above only and not beneath. I am blessed coming in and blessed going out. I am blessed in the city and blessed in the country. He has commanded the blessing to be on my storehouse and on all that I undertake. Why in the world would I be worried that He could not get it to me?

He said in Proverbs that the king's heart is like the watercourses; God directs it wherever He chooses. If He can direct a king's heart, a man who typically believes he is calling the shots, why would He not be able to move on anyone else who is less in rank?

Not only that, but God did *not* say, "Give and I will give back to you exactly what you gave." No! He goes far beyond that! He said it would be a good measure, which means it will not be one of the deceptive measuring instruments some of the less scrupulous merchants sometimes used. God would not only keep it honest, but He would press it down so everything possible that could be put in this measure would be there. Shaken together. Running over. There is more here than the measure can contain.

God always multiplies. Always. When you plant a corn seed, you do not go out and harvest one corn seed. You harvest multiplied hundreds.

Take heart, my soul. Your God will supply.

Perfect Peace

> Be anxious for nothing, but in everything, by prayer and supplication with thanksgiving, let your requests be made known unto God. And the peace of God, which passes all understanding, shall keep your heart and minds through Christ Jesus.
>
> Philippians 4:6-7, NKJV

The Apostle Paul made it abundantly clear that there is nothing in this present world that qualifies anyone to be anxious. Instead, we are to bring those temptations for worry to God. And when we cast our care on Him, we are clear of it, and our focus is only on Him. We once again have nothing for which to be anxious. Then we have the peace which God promises.

The believer has peace, therefore, when he is meditating on the things of God. Usually when we hear of meditating, we picture a scene of peace and tranquility. Meditation seems to us, a time of rest and calm. But meditating can be of quite a different nature.

We are constantly meditating on something. What are we meditating on? If we are constantly full of the Word, God's promises to us, we are guaranteed peace. The Bible states, "He will keep him in perfect peace whose mind is steadfast because he trusts in Him," (Psalm 112:7, NIV). So we can clearly see the direct outcome of our meditation when it is in the direction of God.

But what happens when our meditation is drifting in the wrong direction? We have just entered into anxiety, worry, and concern. The very thing the apostle Paul directed us away from! When he wrote this verse, he was not handing out suggestions for a more peaceful life. He was giving a command! And when a command of Scripture is violated, that is, by definition, a sin!

"Oh, no!" you respond, "I'm not sinning! I'm just very concerned about my child. It's natural for parents to worry about their children." I agree. It is natural for the unrighteous to be worried about the cares of life. But we, as believers, are called to be supernatural, *above* the natural. Through the promises Jesus attained for us through His sufferings at Calvary, we no longer operate as those who have no hope. Here is what Peter advised, "Casting all your care upon the Him, for He cares for you," (1 Peter 5:7, NKJV). We are to put our trust in Him. And when we do this act of obedience, He will give us the peace that passes understanding. To understand is a natural action of the mind. When we move above the natural activities of the natural man, God gives us a peace that the natural mind cannot comprehend. What a tremendous gift! What a glorious benefit!

So let's not waste any more time being anxious! Let's cast off the weight of our worry on the Lord and move into the peace He has for our souls.

Quack

> Be self-controlled and alert. Your enemy the Devil prowls around like a roaring lion looking for someone to devour. Resist him, standing firm in your faith.
>
> 1 Peter 5: 8-9, NIV

My friend, Lindsay, related the following story to me about an incident that happened during her childhood. It seems her family had an eccentric neighbor next door who had a tendency to choose peculiar pets for her family. (This story won't deal with the 500 tadpoles she put in her pool. That story is for another time.) This particular situation has to do with the three ducks she put in her backyard. Now Lindsay's family owned two eighty-pound dogs named Switch and Blade, and they lived in Lindsay's backyard. On the other side of the fence the three ducks quacked loudly, constantly, and pretty much randomly, and it drove this pair of dogs crazy.

One day, circumstances came together to create the perfect storm. Lindsay's family had left the house for the day, and the ducks were up to their daily quacking. Somewhere amidst this racket, it was one quack too many for Blade. He had had enough. I think if we could have heard him speak, he would have said something like, "If I hear one more quack . . ." or "If I have to come over there . . ."

Whatever his thought process was, it drove him to action. He dug under the fence, tunneled his way into the neighbor's backyard, and, let's just say, the quacking stopped. When Lindsay's family returned home, they found their neighbor holding a badly injured duck, heading to the animal hospital. The next day Lindsay's dad poured concrete alongside the edge of the fence to prevent any further tragedy.

This story brought to mind something we all face as Christians trying to keep our focus on living the way Jesus taught us. Sometimes it seems that all we hear is a constant clamoring trying to derail our lives. And we just want peace.

One of the things that seems to quack at us is the world's system. We are constantly bombarded with the pressure to conform to an ever-changing set of social norms that tells us what to think, how to act, what to buy, how to dress, etc, and it's all mixed up in the muddy waters of "there are no absolutes; your truth is what you choose to believe."

Our flesh, our sinful nature, also takes up the chorus of non-stop quacking. It is constantly telling us, "If it feels good, do it." The quacking translation of this mantra goes something like this, "Feed me, pamper me, entertain me, give me everything I lust for, don't hold anything back." I saw a young woman out in public that had an example of this quacking tattooed right on her foot. It read, "Do the don'ts."

Finally, the Devil, whom the Bible calls "the accuser of the brethren", is a professional quacker. He comes to get us off the Word, out of faith, and out of God's plan. His quacks sound something like this, "God doesn't love you. You'll never make it. It seems like you just get ahead, and something else hits you." Or, "See, you did that again. You said you were going to quit and you keep falling into the same old habits and sins. You'll never change. Blah, blah, blah. Quack, quack, quack."

If you can relate to any of these scenarios, it's time to take a lesson from Blade. He decided that putting his paws over his ears was no way to live. He needed to take action. He knew he was an eighty-pound digging machine and he had what it took to change his situation. That's the key: knowing who you are and what you have. The truth is, if you belong to Christ, you have authority over the world, the flesh, and the Devil. You also have God's power to back it up.

When it comes to dealing with the *world*, the Lord told us, "Come out from among them and be you separate," (2 Corinthians 6:17, NKJV). Paul said, "Do not conform to the pattern of this world, but be transformed by the renewing of your mind," (Romans 12:2, NIV).

When the *flesh* is kicking up a ruckus, Paul reminds us, "Walk in the Spirit and you shall not fulfill the lust of the flesh," (Galatians 5:16, NKJV).

And when the *Devil* is busily bringing accusations and temptations to us, James admonishes us, "Submit yourselves, then to God. Resist the Devil, and he will flee from you." (James 4:7, NIV).

Psalm 46:10 says, "Be still and know that I am God," (NKJV). God desires for us to shut out all those voices that are vying for our attention and be quiet before Him. He wants us to hear His voice which will strengthen our spirits and give direction to our lives. Only then will we be able to truly live for Him and bring Him glory.

How about you? Are you getting tired of all that quacking? Are you getting your fill of defeat? Are you feeling like your life has no purpose because you are consumed with holding your paws over your ears? Decide today that you have heard one quack too many. Get digging (into the Word, that is) and get some peace in your life. It sure worked for Blade.

He that Dwelleth

> He that dwelleth in the secret place of the Most High shall abide under the shadow of the Almighty.
>
> Psalm 91:1, KJV

* * * * * * *

Through David, God instructs us to live in the secret place. What is the significance of the secret place? It is God's Presence. Jesus would often go to solitary places to be alone with His Father. He would get up early in the morning before anyone else was stirring, and steal off to an isolated place to have uninterrupted, undistracted time with the Father. The Biblical account shows us He was seeking direction about such weighty matters as whom He should call to be His twelve disciples. Jesus was not only seeking direction from the Father, but also times of intimate fellowship with Him.

The secret place is mentioned in other places in the Bible. Psalm 18:11 says, "He (God) made darkness His secret place," (KJV). What this means is that there are parts of God, characteristics about Him, which are hidden from the knowledge of the world. There are mysteries that have yet to be revealed. Looking at the relationship between these two verses, it looks as though this is the only place where God reveals hidden things about Himself.

No child of the world has access to this knowledge, nor would he understand it if you were to explain it to him. Jesus said these things were hidden from them, but kept for you. Psalm 25:14 reads, "The secret of the LORD is with them that fear Him," (KJV). This Scripture is referring to those believers who seek God. The book of Jeremiah says, "You will seek Me and find Me when you seek Me with all your heart," (Jeremiah 29:13, NIV).

Are you getting this? The God of the Universe, the One who created everything seen and unseen, the Master Mind behind every intricate, delicate detail of the world, states if you want Him to share Who He is with you, you simply make your dwelling, your lifestyle, the very essence of who you are, with Him. He has a storehouse of treasure He wants to share with you, but you must meet the conditions.

The *secret place* is also mentioned in Psalm 139:15, "My frame was not hidden from You when I was made in the secret place," (NIV). He formed your body in the secret place of your mother's womb; and He wants to form you into His image in His secret place. Just as the pre-born baby must spend nine months in its mother's womb, in her very presence, to be ready for the world he or she is preparing to enter, so you too must spend time, day after day, year after year, in the presence of your Heavenly Father, to prepare you for the world you are entering each day. Just as the babe in the womb must have sufficient nourishment each day to develop properly, so you must have the nourishment of fellowship in the Word with your Father. This is the only way to be developed to properly live out the will of God for your life.

Make time to get into the secret place today. It will keep you sheltered for the time to come and get you better acquainted with your loving Father.

Dwelling in the Shelter

> Whoever dwells in the shelter of the Most High will rest in the shadow of the Almighty.
>
> Psalm 91:1, NIV

David had been the leader of his band of men and knew well the dangers of war. He had known the presence and intimacy of God in hard and frightening moments and truly understood that God was as important to survival as taking shelter in the shade when the sun is at its hottest. David was writing out of his experience of trusting in the Lord. He had seen the Lord come to his aid in the direst of circumstances.

Looking at the life of David, one can easily draw the conclusion that David was a man who sought God constantly over the course of his life. He was not one to use God as a last resort. David didn't just live for himself and then call on God when his life was spinning out of control. David had a living, thriving relationship with God. He was dwelling in the shelter of the Most High God.

When you need to stay in a hotel, if you are like me, you travel light and bring as little as you need for the duration. Even if you stay for two weeks, you don't move all of your possessions in and tell everyone that the hotel is your new address. You are not **dwelling** at the hotel; you are just staying there temporarily.

The book of James tells us the Word of God is a mirror for our lives. If we use this Scripture to get a good look at our lives, we would have to ask, "Is my relationship with God just a hotel stay or is it my permanent address?" The answer to this question would determine whether or not the second part of this verse applies to us. If we are not dwelling in constant relationship with God, then we will not be able to rest in the shadow of the Almighty.

What does this mean? Well, to rest in the shadow of a tree, a person has to be close to the tree. As much as you might wish to be in the shade of a tree on a hot day, if you are across the field from it, its shadow will not make any change in your situation. Now, if the tree is yours, or you have permission to be there, and you are willing to do what it takes to get there, you can enjoy the benefits of the shade. But with God, the conditions are slightly different. Just as you don't let just anyone come into your house, God has requirements for those who need to be close to Him. To put it in a nutshell, sin separates us from God.

So if we desire to enjoy fellowship with Him, we must obey the conviction of the Holy Spirit when He shows us where we have left the path. If we are willing to do what it takes to get in the place of relationship with God, we will enjoy the beauty of being in His Presence.

So get in your shelter and enjoy some rest. God will meet you there.

Under the Shadow

Abide under the shadow of the Almighty.

Psalm 91:1, KJV

* * * * * * *

What is the significance of a shadow? To be in the shadow of something denotes closeness. In order to enjoy the shade of a tree, you must be somewhat close to the trunk. So it is with God. If you just check in with Him at Christmas and Easter services, (I've heard this type of church character is called a Chreaster), and expect God to answer your prayers in a desperate situation, you will be waiting a long time. You must have an abiding relationship with Him daily.

The shadow also speaks of relief or protection. If you are caught in a rainstorm, you would probably enjoy the benefit of being under the "shadow" of an umbrella. This shadow protects you from the effects of the rain. If you had to trudge out in a dry, hot place for hours, you would appreciate the cooling shade of a parasol. So, it seems to be me, a benefit of dwelling in the secret place of God is that you get to abide under the shadow of the Almighty. Or to put it another way, a condition for abiding under the shadow of the Almighty is that you are first of all dwelling in the secret place of the Most High. In other words, there is a price to pay for the benefit of abiding in the protection of the shadow.

The relationship you have with God is so important. So many times we take our relationship with God for granted and, as a result, we treat it so casually. While we are busy pampering our flesh and not making the sacrifices necessary to have a thriving fellowship with God, we are unknowingly placing ourselves in a very dangerous position. We have left ourselves completely unprotected in a world that is hostile to us. Once we have repented and submitted ourselves to the Lordship of Jesus, we have, for all practical purposes, painted a big, red target on ourselves. I Peter 5:8 says, "your adversary, the Devil, as a roaring lion, walks about, seeking whom he may devour," (NKJV). And Satan will take every opportunity afforded to him to destroy us.

I don't think David was casually tossing out a suggestion to us as an alternative to our monotony when he wrote these passionate words. I don't think he was saying, "Hey, if you get a spare moment sometime, (I know how busy you are), you might try getting together with God." No! He was laying down a principle, a truth. "If you have a living relationship with a living God, here is what will happen to your life." He left the obvious alternative for you to figure out. But in case you don't see it, here it is. If you choose not to be in God's presence on a daily basis, you will not abide in His protection. There is no gray area. There are only two options. The choice is up to you.

I Will Say of the Lord

> And I will say of the LORD, "He is my refuge, and my fortress, my God, in Him will I trust."
>
> Psalm 91:2, NIV

David made the above statement, "And I will say of the Lord . . ." In making this statement, he was declaring a decision, a choice. This is a statement of his will, "I *will say* . . ." He was informing his will, "This is the direction we are going." In essence his spirit was taking charge of his will. On the flip side, he was also directing that his will did not have the option to turn away from the Lord.

To whom was he speaking? Himself! He was using the power of his words to direct himself. He was saying, "Self, here is what we are going to do in the face of danger and affliction. We are going to declare that God is our refuge, our fortress, and our God. In Him will we trust." David was saying in the face of danger God was a more secure refuge than any cave, mountain, forest, or any other place in which he could hide. God was to him a fortress, a wall of protection around him. He was declaring that God Almighty was his God, the focus of his worship and sustenance.

David also declared it was in God that he would trust, not in David's ability to do whatever was in his power to do. He would not put his trust in his own strength or the 600 men with him and their ability to fight for him. He was only trusting in the all-sustaining and almighty power of his God to preserve him. He had been dwelling in the secret place of the Most High and had been abiding under the shadow of the Almighty. Now he was making a vocal declaration and I believe he really did not care who heard him.

This all sounds very poetic to us and we applaud David's courage and boldness. But, fellow believer, how does this apply to you? When you are facing a dangerous sickness or a scary shortfall in financial matters, do you make such a declaration? Many times, when that hideous voice of fear begins to whisper in your ear that you are not going to make it this time, that bad things have happened in the past but this is the worst, that this sickness has hung on a long time and seems to be getting more serious all the time, etc. you feel completely defeated. You know what I am talking about. The words come flying into your mind faster than you can process them, much less answer them with any semblance of your faith being intact. What can you do?

Just what David did! Let your spirit, that born-again part of you that has been taking in the Word of God, take charge. Shut down all of that mess in your mind. Your mind is processing all of the facts presented to you. And the facts are not pretty. So close that off for now. Address your will. Tell your will which direction you are going to move. Do not let fear be the deciding factor for your will. Put the Word of God on the throne of your will and do not let circumstances dethrone it from its rightful place. Present to your mind the truths that are a higher priority to you, "He is my refuge, my fortress, my God. In Him will I trust." When your will and mind have gotten into line behind your spirit, your emotions will fall right in step. Then you will have an undivided heart and you will have positioned yourself for victory in the Lord. Charles Spurgeon said, "To trust God is the sure way to every blessing, and He is worthy of the most implicit confidence." (Morning & Evening, p.269) Amen!

Snare of the Fowler

> Surely He will deliver you from the snare of the fowler and from the noisesome pestilence. He shall cover you with His feathers, and under His wings shall you trust.
>
> Psalm 91:3-4, AKJV

When the believer trusts in God and draws close to His heart, he can then lay claim to these promises. God will deliver the believer who has met the condition of being in close fellowship with Him. When you, friend, are leaning your head in the bosom of your Savior, you will hear His voice speaking through His Spirit warning you of danger. When you think about the snare of the fowler, you will see how completely necessary this facet of God's protection is. When a fowler, one who hunts birds, goes about his job of throwing a net over his prey, he must be very sneaky. In another place in Scripture, it reads, "How useless to spread a net in full view of all the birds!" (NIV). The fowler makes it his business to be undetected when hunting birds.

This is quite a chilling thought when viewed in the light of our situation. To think that you are a bird, and your enemy, Satan, is the fowler hunting you, well, you can see how much need you have of One who sees all and is also your Deliverer. As you walk along the path of your life, Satan comes as a roaring lion seeking whom he may devour. He watches the predictability of your life, and sets a snare, hoping to deter you from God's will. But God, because of His great love for you and because of His planned purpose, pulls you away from that trap as you are walking in obedience to Him. As you walk in close fellowship with Him, He is able to move on your behalf.

On the contrary, if you have distanced yourself from your Savior because of your self will and disobedience, you have moved off the path and sure disaster awaits you. If this is your situation, simply repent. Get things right with God and get back on His path for your life.

Look more closely to see what else God promises to do for you. "He will cover you with His feathers and under His wings will you trust." Wow! Not only will God deliver you from the fowler, He will cover you with His feathers! Stop for a moment and visualize this scene. A little bird has just alighted in an open place. He does not notice the net beneath his tiny feet. The fowler is about to draw the net together to bag his prey. But suddenly there is the sound of a mighty rushing wind. An enormous shadow passes over this miniscule creature. The bulk of a huge bird alights over the little one and encompasses it with its gargantuan wings. The Deliverer has arrived on the scene. The fowler tries in vain to pull the snare. The little bird is free. The enemy has been put to flight.

Stay close to your Deliverer! He is ready and willing to help you!

The Truth of God

His truth shall be your shield and buckler.

Psalm 91:4, NKJV

The truth of God, when employed by a believer whose faith is intact, will never fail to bring about protection and victory. The soldier's shield was used to protect the vital organs, especially the heart. God's truth will always protect our hearts from the lies, deceptions, and manipulations of the devil. But the shield must be in place. It does your heart no good when the enemy is breathing lies to your heart and your Bible is lying on your coffee table. The truth will do no good unless it is grasped and held in place. You must be handling the word of truth in order for the protection to be there.

In Ephesians 6, the apostle Paul told us that the shield is actually the Shield of Faith. When the truth is present, but is not being held out with the hand of faith, unbelief will throw it down to the ground. The heart then, is wide open to the flaming arrows of the enemy of our souls. Many times we are hit with an open attack from our adversary, and immediately our thoughts fly to *What is going on here, God?* A simple check in the mirror, the Word of God, will reveal to us the state of our armor. We need to simply adjust our armor, which means we immerse ourselves in the Word, renew our minds to its ways, and become transformed.

The other part of the above Scripture text is the term *buckler*. A buckler was a belt used by warriors to strap their weapons to them. Similar in its purpose to a carpenter's tool belt, the buckler was used to keep the weapons "at the ready". When one is engaged in brutal hand-to-hand combat, there is no time to be searching through a collection of weapons to find the right one. The soldier, therefore, had to be familiar with each weapon, recognize its purpose, and know quickly where it was on the buckler in order to have it at his disposal.

Likewise, our buckler of truth should have hanging from it promises from God's Word. As soldiers of light, we need to train ourselves in the promises of the Word. Paul told us, "Study to show yourself approved unto God, a workman that needs not to be ashamed, rightly dividing the word of truth," (2 Timothy 2:15, NKJV). We need to be trained to handle the Word rightly. No one would send an untrained man as a soldier into the fray. That man would do more harm than good to the cause. It behooves us as believers to find the promises that Satan is challenging in our lives, memorize them, meditate on them, and be bold to resist the Devil with them. Then we will see the victory God had intended for us.

Lessons from an Elephant

> Submit yourselves, then, to God. Resist the devil and he will flee from you.
>
> James 4:7, NIV

I heard a story many years ago about a nature photographer who hired some bush men in Africa to accompany him. He wanted to get pictures of individual members of a certain herd of elephants. At one point, the bush men had him hide with them behind some bushes to observe the movements of the herd. They could see a strong bull elephant coming to the fore. This particular elephant began to wave his trunk toward the bushes in an aggressive manner. The bush men looked bewildered. Why was this elephant behaving this way?

Because of the distance from which they were viewing the animals, one of the bush men pulled out binoculars to have a look. Much to their amazement, as the bull elephant frantically waved his trunk and gave warning to the group, they noticed a tiny baby elephant had made his way to the space just between the bull elephant's front legs. The baby began to wave his trunk at the group as well. But somehow this little guy was sending a different message to the men. His gesture seemed to be communicating something along the lines of, "Ha ha ha ha ha ha" sung to the tune of "Ring Around the Rosy". He seemed to be mocking them. He was saying, "It doesn't really matter how dangerous you might be; my daddy is bigger than all of you put together!"

So what does this have to do with you and me and our walk with God? Plenty! Just as these bush men and this photographer could have posed a threat to this baby elephant, and therefore be considered an enemy, we too have a real threat in this world, namely Satan. One huge danger is our ignorance of him. For our purposes here, we will agree that Satan is real. Once we are aware of this peril, we need to be ever vigilant as to his operation in our lives. The bull elephant was highly alert for potential dangers. His response was one of resistance. He took a stand and said, with his actions, "You will come this far and no further. If you do come further, you will face severe consequences."

Let's look at the baby. Did he seem fearful or worried? Not at all! To the contrary, the baby was extremely confident. Why? Because he knew with certainty that his daddy would handle any potential dangers with no problem. This is a great picture of our Heavenly Father. When Satan begins to move toward us to attack us, our Father begins to move to protect His children. One thing to keep in mind though, is that we have to remain under God's protection. If that baby elephant had run out away from the bull elephant, his protection would have vanished. When we stay in the "secret place of the Most High" we "shall abide under the shadow of the Almighty," (Ps 91:1, NKJV). In order to stay protected we must have a trusting relationship with our Heavenly Father.

So, the next time you see an elephant, remember God's protection. It really is a big thing.

If God Be For Us

If God be for us, who can be against us?

> Romans 8:31, KJV

Have you ever felt you are doing everything you can to follow God, yet everything in your life seems to be cursed? I have hit one of those times. In prayer today I was just honest with God. I told Him when I look around me, it seems as if other Christians I know seem to be getting blessed out of measure, and yet I keep plugging away, holding on to my faith, not looking at circumstances, keeping my eyes on the Scripture. Life just seems to be one constant uphill battle with no relief in sight. It also seems as if God answers the prayers of some while others go unheeded. I know in my heart this is not true, so I asked God why it looked this way.

When I got finished baring my heart to Him, I heard two things. The first was this: "Stir yourself up". God was showing me that my fire of belief has died way down. Yes, there is still heat present, but no flames were evident. I need to get my confessions going again. I need to let my born-again spirit take the lead and generate some fervent prayers again. I had gradually let my mind talk me out of what my spirit knows to be true. The prayers I was muttering didn't even come close to convincing my mind that I believed it. I needed to take up the weapons of my warfare and march boldly into battle. The lyrics of a recent song proclaim, "We will cross over Jordan. We will claim what You've promised." I had to get the spirit of a warrior back into my soul.

I need to put on the full armor of God: the helmet of salvation—a guard over my mind; the breastplate of righteousness—a guard over my heart; waist girdled with truth—a guard against being deceived; feet shod with the readiness of the peace of the Gospel—a firm stability that does not give up ground to the enemy; the sword of the Spirit—the Word of God; and the shield of faith that quenches every fiery dart of the wicked—taking down the attacks of the Devil before they can do any damage.

The other word the Lord spoke to me was *unbelief*. I had just learned in church that one definition of *unbelief* means "having the perspective of the Devil." God showed me that when I was entertaining the thought, *This sickness seems like it will never go away*, what I was really doing was thinking the Devil's thoughts after him. When I was thinking, *We always seem to struggle financially and never get ahead*, I was pondering the Devil's perspective.

What a wake-up call! I know the Devil speaks the language of lies and everything he says is twisted. Then why did I repeat his "faith" confessions instead of God's? I had to be reminded of the verse above "If God be for me, who can be against me!" If I get my mind completely in God's camp, I will not only stop shooting myself in the foot, I will begin firing at the enemy and will see victory in short order. To God be the praise!

The Chicken and the Banana Peel

> And He said to them, "Take heed and beware of covetousness: for a man's life consists not in the abundance of the things which he possesses."
>
> Luke 12:15, AKJV

I changed my normal morning walking routine to take a detour into the chicken coop. My oldest daughter, whose job it is to open up the coop every morning, was off on her first mission trip, so I volunteered for the job. As I stood back from the little trap door I had just opened, I thought about how cute the chickens looked as each one in turn hopped out and began its daily duty of pecking at grass and bugs. I was just about to leave the scene, when I sensed the Lord detaining me. I knew I was in store for something, so I just stood there in anticipation.

I was not disappointed. I soon spotted a hen who had found an abandoned banana peel. She picked it up and began to run. Not being a discreet creature, she soon attracted the attention of several other hens. They ran round and round until, finally, a faster hen snatched it and ran away. Then the chase began again with the new hen. She ran until a fast rooster snatched it and gobbled as fast as he could. Before long, the banana peel was nothing more than a memory.

I stood there, trying to grasp what the Lord was teaching me. I believe the Lord was illustrating for me how silly our worthless pursuits of this world's treasures are. We run around trying to grasp what we think is so important in this life, and once we get it, we run around tirelessly trying to protect it and keep it from others. But, as Solomon pointed out in Ecclesiastes, it is really meaningless and a chasing after the wind. What looks so silly played out by a flock of chickens and a worthless piece of garbage is how we live a good portion of our lives. God has a much more significant purpose for our existence. He wants us to live lives full of the Holy Spirit, telling others about Jesus, and glorifying Him. But we are so busy raking straw and dirt like the old man in Pilgrim's Progress. Christian was being taught some important lesson by the Interpreter. To quote the book:

". . .a man was raking a pile of straw and dirt. Before him stood another man who held out a crown. But the raker would not take the crown. 'The riches of this world are like straw and dirt,' said the Interpreter. 'This man would rather have them than an eternal crown.'"

We must keep our focus on Jesus and not on the things of this world. Jesus Himself said that a man's life does not consist in the abundance of his possessions. He also said that a man could gain the whole world and yet lose his soul. Here is what I found in Isaiah 2:7-8 concerning the house of Jacob:

> Their land is full of silver and gold;
> There is no end to their treasures.
> Their land is full of horses;
> There is no end to their chariots.

> Their land is full of idols;
> They bow down to the work of their hands,
> To what their fingers have made. (NIV)

You see what this passage says? By the time Israel got full of their treasures, they had turned into idolaters. They had gotten so full of their stuff, that they ended up being full of themselves.

So hold your earthly treasures loosely. Pursue those things that have eternal significance.

And don't be a chicken.

Above All Else Guard Your Heart

> Above all else, guard your heart, for it is the wellspring of life. Put away perversity from your mouth; keep corrupt talk far from your lips.
>
> Proverbs 4: 23-24, NIV

I've been thinking much about how the Word of God is a seed which is to be planted in our hearts. In Mark 4:26, Jesus says, "This is what the Kingdom of God is like. A man scatters seed on the ground," (NIV). When I was looking at the above Scripture, I saw this truth once again. My heart is the *garden* of who I am. So if I plant the seed of God's Word in my heart I will have the fruit of this seed coming up in my life. But on the other hand, if I plant bad seed or, just as bad, if I don't keep watch over what is being planted in my heart, I will have the harvest from that seed as well.

What jumped out at me in the above verse is the two ways I could allow a destructive harvest into my life. "Put away perversity from your mouth." Obviously, I should not speak blatantly immoral ideas out of my mouth. But it is actually far more reaching than that. God does not want me speaking anything contrary to His Word because, just by its very nature in being contrary to God, it is perverse. So if God says you are loved by Him and you say, in times of trial especially, that God doesn't care about you, that statement is perverse. John 3:16 says God so loved you that He sent His Son to die for you. If you feel sick and you believe God put this ailment on you, that idea is perverse. Isaiah 53:5-6 says that the punishment that brought us peace was upon Jesus and by His stripes we are healed.

The next part of the verse above says, "Keep corrupt talk far from your lips." If I want to keep the garden of my heart clear of weeds, then I cannot speak negative, hurtful, critical, slanderous, blasphemous words out of my mouth. I cannot afford to spit these dangerous seeds around the soil of my heart. The consequences are completely destructive.

Proverbs 4 tells me I need to guard my heart above all else, for out of it proceeds the issues of life. I need to plant the right things in this garden, keep the weeds out, and then guard it more than anything else. I can then expect at harvest time to see the blessings of God flourishing in my life.

The Worth of a Donkey

> You are worthy, O Lord, to receive glory and honor and power . . .
>
> Revelation 4:11, NKJV

A dozen or so years ago, I was at a yard sale and I dug around in one of those "miscellaneous" boxes. It had a sign which read, "Items in box 50 cents". I found a small blue planter in the shape of a donkey. It was cute so I brought it home and gave it a place on my kitchen window sill.

Recently, I happened to be antiquing and found an identical donkey planter with the exception that this one was plum-colored instead of blue. I was eager to see the price at which this planter was valued and was pleasantly surprised. It was marked twenty-five dollars! You can bet that now when I look at my yard sale donkey I see it with new eyes. What used to be just a fifty-cent trinket is now a valuable antique. How many times have you seen the antiques show featuring someone who found something at a yard sale for a few dollars only to have the expert inform him that it is worth tens of thousands of dollars?

This lends itself to several interesting questions. First, how do I value God? Before I was born again, God was not at the top of my priority list. I believed that He existed but I was not serving Him. Until I understood that I needed to repent and turn to Him and live His way, I did not appreciate His worth. But after I got saved, I was able to look at God with new eyes. I saw how majestic and glorious and worthy of praise He is.

Second, how do I value the things of God? For instance, is the Bible just a nice little addition to the windowsill of my life? Is it just something nice to have, but has no real value in my life? Or maybe some experience or trial has given me a new perspective on how valuable God's Word is in my life and now I see that I could not live without God's truth penetrating my heart.

Third, how do I value prayer? In my younger Christian days, I saw it as a necessary discipline, but as the years have gone by and answered prayer has impacted my life, I began to see the treasure and privilege that prayer is. Something that I had in my possession all along suddenly seemed tremendously more valuable.

So, as you are learning new truths about God, His Word, and prayer, try not to look on them as devalued trinkets. Just because someone else might have thrown one or more of these things aside and did not ascribe value to them, don't be too quick to devalue them. Don't throw away a valuable treasure. It will change your life.

The God of the Impossible

> The things which are impossible with men are possible with God.
>
> Luke 18:27, NKJV

Do you have something in your life that seems completely impossible? Were you tooling along life's path just fine and a roadblock got thrown in your way? That's what happened to Moses and the Israelites at the Red Sea. At the last minute, God parted the Red Sea and let the Israelites pass through on dry ground. The interesting thing is that the deliverance was only for them. As soon as they were on dry ground, God allowed the waters of the Red Sea to flow back together and drown the Egyptians. Why?

In II Chronicles 20 Jehoshaphat and Judah found themselves surrounded by three armies. There was no escape. But Jehoshaphat cried out to God for deliverance and the armies turned on each other and were destroyed. Why?

Hannah desperately wanted a baby. Up until now, she had born the disgrace of being barren. God granted her request and soon she held a bouncing baby boy. Other women in her day were barren and stayed barren. Why?

There were dozens of people thronging Jesus the day that the woman with the issue of blood received deliverance from her infirmity. Many of those people had urgent needs as well, but only she got her need met. Why?

At least 2 reasons. In Luke 18:27 Jesus said, "The things which are impossible with men are possible with God," (KJV). God is well able to do the impossible. So why doesn't He do the impossible for just anyone?

Because Hebrews 11:6 says that "without faith it is impossible to please Him: for he that cometh to God must believe that He is, and that He is a rewarder of them that diligently seek Him," (KJV).

If we want God to move on our behalf, we must have faith in Him. We must not let ourselves be deceived by a superficial or emotional lather we work ourselves into. Romans 10 says, "Faith comes by hearing and hearing by the Word of God," (NKJV). We get faith by getting into God's Word and understanding His character.

Moses and the Israelites had faith in God to deliver them and they received their miracle. Jehoshaphat and Judah trusted God to deliver them from their enemies and they received their miracle. Hannah trusted God and received her little miracle. The woman with the issue of blood had faith in Jesus and received her miracle.

So what is your Red Sea today? What armies have surrounded you that are whispering your doom? What is barren or dead in your life that needs to be resurrected? What plague is draining your hopes and dreams?

Give it to God in faith. And watch Him do the impossible.

Faith and Grace

> For it is by grace you have been saved, through faith--
> and this not from yourselves, it is the gift of God.
>
> Ephesians 2:8, NIV

I've been trying to understand the role of grace in my faith walk. I have thought that what God does in my life completely depends on what I do and what shape my faith is in. This put a tremendous burden on me to make sure I was living right. But where is the line to cross that would show that I was living right enough? Because this is an ambiguous area, Satan has a perfect setup when I am putting my faith on the line for something, to put condemnation on me, telling me that I don't deserve to have my prayers answered. This then opens the door for doubt to take root. The first chapter of James tells us that if we are in doubt, or double-minded, we will receive nothing from the Lord. So what are we to do?

I have been coming to understand better how this works. First we have to understand about our covenant purchased by the blood of Jesus. According to the Bible, Jesus redeemed everything for us that God had originally placed in the Garden of Eden. This includes health, prosperity, righteousness, holiness, every good and perfect gift that God could give. This covenant cannot be broken and is our rightful inheritance as adopted sons of God. This is our "blessing".

The blessing in the Bible was symbolized by rivers and pools. In agricultural societies, rivers and pools were necessary for survival. Egypt was established by the Nile River because it offered abundant prosperity for growing crops and raising livestock. St. Louis, Nashville, and any number of cities were founded beside rivers for the same reason, not to mention the added benefit of travel. So the blessing represents an abundance of life.

The opposite, however, is the absence of life-giving water. Drought, famine, disease, and death are all natural consequences of the "curse". Let's say, for instance, that a farmer has just bought a new farm. It has a nice house and barn, good soil, and a creek running right through the middle of the fields. All is going well: the fields have been cultivated and planted and the livestock is coming along well. What the farmer doesn't know is that his neighbor upstream has decided to create a lake out of the creek, so he dams up the water and now the farmer has only a dry creek bed. His farm is now facing hard times—no water for the animals or fields. He could potentially lose everything he invested in. He is, essentially, "cursed".

Now, the book of Galatians tells us that Jesus has redeemed us from the curse of the law. We are no longer under the curse that became reality in this world as a result of Adam's sin. Everything that Adam "earned" for us is no longer in effect for our lives. So what is the problem? Why do our lives not seem to reflect this state of affairs? Because we have an enemy who is also a deceiver. If Satan can use deception to talk us out of our inheritance, we will live as if we have no covenant.

This reminds me of the scene in *Pilgrim's Progress* when Christian and a friend find themselves thrown into the Dungeon of Despair. They had sat in the darkness of that place for hours on end, depressed and wondering how things would turn out. Suddenly one of them touched something on the dungeon floor they had not noticed before. It was a key! Yes, the dungeon had been locked. Yes, they had been down there for days! But the truth was, they would not have had to spend one second in that place because their freedom had been provided for all along.

The same is true for us. Yes, we may be battling a health, financial, or relational issue. Yes, it looks hopeless or maybe we have been battling it for years. But the truth is, we do not have to spend one more second in that place because our freedom has already been provided for.

This "provision" is what grace is all about. Through the grace of God, not only has our salvation been provided for, but also everything that Jesus purchased at Calvary! Our faith is merely the tool we use to access what God has already provided by grace. Our faith is not a means to get God to do what we are praying for; it is merely the vehicle to access what is already ours. If you have a checking account, and if you have written a check lately, you understand that the check is not actually the money. Nor is the check a means of strong-arming the bank into giving you money. Rather, you are trying to access the money that was put there. In this case, God deposited the money out of His unlimited account by His grace!

So, if you are believing God, say, for healing, then you pray in faith believing God for what has already been provided in the spiritual realm to manifest in the physical realm. Hebrews 11:1 says, "Faith is the substance of things hoped for, the evidence of things not seen," (NKJV). We hope for the manifestation of what has already been provided for; it just hasn't been seen yet. The same verse in the Amplified Bible states, "things not perceived by the five senses." If you are looking at your body full of symptoms of sickness to see how your faith is doing, you will never find your faith. It is only perceived spiritually. "We live by faith, not by sight," (2 Corinthians 5:7, NIV).

If we believed for salvation by faith the same way we try to believe God for other aspects of the covenant, we would probably never get saved. We would be begging God to save us, instead of receiving the salvation He had already provided. Faith is a tool that works the same way every time. We must use faith to access by grace everything provided in our blessing. We must use our faith on purpose to get not only ourselves free but, like Christian in the Dungeon, those around us as well.

Disappointment

> Whoever believes in Him will not be disappointed.
>
> Romans 10:11, NASB

A young paratrooper was learning to jump. He was given the following instructions: "First, jump when you are told; second, count to ten and pull the ripcord; third, in the very unlikely event that it doesn't open, pull the second chute open; and fourth, when you get down, a truck will take you back to the base." The plane ascended up to the proper height, the men started peeling out, and the young paratrooper jumped when told. He counted to ten and pulled the cord, but the chute failed to open. He proceeded to the back-up plan: he pulled the cord of the second chute. It, too, failed to open. "And I suppose," he complained to himself, "the truck won't be there either when I get down."

Do you have some dream or expectation that just seems to be going nowhere? In the middle of this disappointment, do you find yourself questioning God's wisdom or even His love for you? Have you gone beyond questioning Him and are now bitter towards Him for not fulfilling your expectations?

I believe one reason why we get disappointed with events in our lives is that we get so focused on our own deal. We forget that this life is about God and not us, if we have truly submitted our hearts to Him. If Jesus is our Lord, we should spend ourselves asking Him what it is that *He* wants and not worry about ourselves. If we could step back and see *why* God allowed our plan to fall through, we would see the loving heart of our Father at work.

Okay, now I might offend some of you out there, so remember that you are supposed to love me in the Lord. I've got to get this off my chest. You have all seen the "God is my co-pilot" bumper sticker. Well, I have a problem with that. God is *not* my co-pilot! He owns all of the airlines! He is in charge of this thing! We get disappointed because we are steering this plane and we really don't know which way is best. But He has graciously allowed us to ride along with Him on this journey and serve Him! When He turns the plane in another direction, we have to trust that He knows what He's doing.

Maybe there is a severe storm that could bring us down, and He's taking us around it. Or maybe the entire flight got cancelled because the plane would have crashed. There are countless reasons God doesn't give us what we were expecting, and He'll either explain it here or in heaven, but one thing is for sure: He does love us. Romans 8:28 says, "And we know that in all things God works for the good of those who love Him, who have been called according to His purpose," (NIV).

Since God is *the* pilot, you might want to move over into the passenger seat and let Him have the controls. You won't be disappointed.

Singing in the Rain

Rejoice in the Lord always. I will say it again. Rejoice!

Philippians 4:4, NIV

A few days ago I woke up to rain. I had been going through an extended trial and it just would have been cheering to wake up to sunshine. But I propped myself up in my bed and grabbed my Bible. As I began to study and get into the story of my daily reading, the quiet sound of the rain captured my attention. There was something lingering behind the gentle drumming. What was it? Then I realized—it was songbirds! Why were songbirds sitting out in this rain, singing?

I pondered this for a moment. Then it hit me. Spring had finally blossomed and, even though the sky was gloomy and the rain was pouring in sad torrents, these birds couldn't hold back. They just had to let all that exuberance out. These happy creatures just couldn't contain this joy any longer. They had to sing out into all creation, and especially to their Creator, the thankfulness in their little hearts for spring's arrival.

How about you? How do you react when the skies of your life are gloomy and the rain is coming down in sheets? Is your focus on the depressing atmosphere and what you wish your circumstances were? Or do you look at what God has shown you by His promises in the Word about your future?

It is so important to remind ourselves not to focus on what is wrong or what we've lost, but instead to look at what we have, what God has so graciously blessed us with. Psalm 50:23 tells us, "He who brings an offering of praise and thanksgiving honors and glorifies Me; and he who orders his way aright (who prepares the way that I may show him) to him I will demonstrate the salvation of God," (AMP). Instead of using the word *offering*, the New American Standard Bible uses the word *sacrifice*, "He who offers a sacrifice of thanksgiving honors Me."

Webster defines sacrifice as "the surrender or destruction of something valued for the sake of something having a higher or more pressing claim". When circumstances threaten to discourage you, it becomes a sacrifice to praise and thank the Lord for the good things you do have in your life. That very surrender of yourself will be the thing that puts you in a position for God to demonstrate His salvation and His deliverance in your situation.

So, the next time it is raining in your heart, open your mouth and let the praises fly out. Spring and sunshine are just around the corner.

Healing & Worship

For the past several years I have been dealing with at least two chronic conditions that have been stubbornly hanging on. I decided that maybe I just didn't know enough to see deliverance. 2 Peter 1:3 says, "His divine power has given us everything required for life and godliness through the knowledge of Him Who called us by His own glory and goodness," (HCSB).

If I believe this verse to be absolutely and completely true, then everything I need for life and godliness has been made available to me by Jesus. These unhealthy conditions plaguing my body do affect my life. Many times I just want to stay in bed because I feel so bad. I know that is not the quality of life Jesus was talking about when He said in John 10:10, "I am come that they might have life and that they might have it more abundantly," (NKJV). Having symptoms of sickness every day is not the abundant life Jesus has planned for me.

Being sick also affects a person's godliness. When you don't feel good day after day, it is very easy to slip into discouragement or grumpiness. I don't see any provision in the Bible anywhere allowing a person to be a grouch just because he or she is sick. Another thing I've noticed is this: when I don't feel well, everything is an uphill climb. I don't feel inclined to witness, or to do any other good deeds when I am hurting. Other people's needs are second place to mine. The raging symptoms command center stage.

So how was I to get back on track with life and godliness? The next part of the Scripture reads, "through our knowledge of Him." Something I've heard one of my favorite ministers say repeatedly is if your prayers seem unanswered, you don't have a faith problem, you have a knowledge problem. "Faith comes by hearing, and hearing by the Word of God," (Romans 10:17, NKJV). Faith has its basis in the Word of God, which is knowledge. So faith has to have a foundation of knowledge on which to build.

I decided that I would need to bone up on the Scripture verses dealing with healing. I read one day in Joshua 1:8, "This book of the law shall not depart out of your mouth, but you shall meditate therein day and night, that you may observe to do according to all that is written therein; for then you shall make your way prosperous and then you shall have good success," (NKJV). In the Amplified version, it actually says, "then you shall deal wisely". Wow! I have been "dealing" with these health issues; I just hadn't been "dealing wisely".

I had to increase my knowledge of Jesus, who is the Word, in order to have some foundation for my faith. This led me to yet another verse in I John 2:20, "But you have an anointing from the Holy One and you know all things," (NKJV). The teaching I heard on this topic pointed me to pray in the Spirit for wisdom. One afternoon recently, I was praying over this situation and feeling particularly rotten physically. The verse in James 1:5 came to my mind, "If any of you lacks wisdom, you should ask God, Who gives generously to all without finding fault, and it will be given to you," (NIV).

"God," I prayed, "please give me wisdom about getting healed. This has gone on way too long." About an hour later, I went to our Wednesday service at church, and the pastor's sermon title was "Faith and Patience" and he majored on James chapter 1. God had my attention. I took copious notes, but still felt that I needed to clarify some of the points with the pastor. I told him about my ongoing situation, and he said, "You can have a lot of knowledge, but if your praise is not in balance with your knowledge and faith, you will struggle."

That night I wrote in my journal what the pastor had said. My journal is one that has a different verse on each page. On the page I came to write on, the verse was James 1:5! Again, God had my attention. A few days later, I once again opened the book I had been reading, "Christ the Healer" by F.F. Bosworth. He was discussing the steps of how to appropriate your healing. He said that you need to incorporate praise into your request to God for healing. Then he went on to say this,

"Faith is what we have before we are healed. 'They shall praise the Lord that *seek* Him. Thou shalt call thy wall salvation, and thy gates praise.' Without praise we are up against a solid wall with no gate; but when we begin praising, and appropriating, we hang our own gate, and walk through. 'Be glad and rejoice for the Lord *will do* great things,' and accordingly, 'they were continually in the Temple praising and blessing God,' not after, but before they were filled with the Holy Spirit. It was 'when they lifted up their voice and praised the Lord' that 'the glory of the Lord filled the House of God.' 'They believed His *words* (not their symptoms, not the "father of lies") and sang His praises.'" (p.99)

I also saw in Psalm 68:1, "God arises and His enemies are scattered. Those who hate Him flee from His presence," (ISV). Psalm 22:3 says, "Yet You are holy, enthroned on the praises of

Israel," (ESV). The understanding I got from putting these two verses of Scripture together was this: when you praise God, He is enthroned on your praises, or another version says "inhabits" the praises of His people. When you praise God, He brings His presence to where you are; He is actually enthroned on your praise. The first Scripture tells us that the enemies of God cannot stand in the His presence. So if you are praising God, His presence invades and drives out your enemies!

I'm going to make sure the scales of praise and Bible knowledge are balanced. And then I'm going get ready for God to make His move!

Broken Pieces

> Taking the five loaves and the two fish and looking up to heaven, He gave thanks and broke the loaves. Then He gave them to His disciples to set before the people. He also divided the two fish among them all. They all ate and were satisfied and the disciples picked up twelve basketfuls of broken pieces of bread and fish. The number of the men who had eaten was five thousand.
>
> Mark 6:41-44, NIV

Jesus had performed a great miracle, something completely unthinkable to the disciples. He had taken a small boy's lunch, a two-piece fish dinner and had multiplied it to the point that five thousand men, not to mention the women and children present, had eaten until they were as stuffed as any good Thanksgiving turkey. And yet the disciples picked up *twelve basketfuls of broken pieces!*

Have you ever asked yourself this question: with the ability Jesus had to produce abundantly more than thousands of people could eat, why did He have the disciples bother with the leftovers? I mean, leave it for the ants! Obviously, Jesus had no problem with a lack of resources in His life. So why gather up the crumbs?

The answer might surprise you. The reason Jesus had the disciples gather the broken pieces of bread and fish is because He never wastes *anything!* Think about it this way: do you have any broken pieces of your life? Are there broken relationships, bad life choices, lost opportunities, regrets? Do you ponder what meaning these could have in your life or what in the world God could do with them?

Well, Jesus, in essence, says, "Gather them up. Leave nothing behind. I want them." Why? Because He can redeem them. How? He can bring healing to those broken areas of your life and then use you as His tool to minister healing to someone else in your life someday. He can use the dark times in your life to bring the light of His glory into someone else's life. As Joseph said, "What you meant for evil, God turned for good."

So start filling your basket. Jesus is ready to multiply blessing in your life.

Looking unto Jesus

Looking unto Jesus, the Author and Finisher of our faith.

Hebrews 12:2, AKJV

* * * * * * *

Have you ever felt like giving up? You have done everything you know to do to change your circumstances and yet they stubbornly refuse to budge. You wonder if God is even paying attention to your situation. Everything that could go wrong has gone wrong. Why even try anymore?

The reason you should not give up is because you have Jesus on your side. God has stated in Genesis, "Is anything too hard for the Lord?" (Genesis 18:14, NIV). Paul tells us in the New Testament that God will not put more on you than you can bear without giving you a way of escape. God wants us to persevere in the race that is set before us, casting aside every weight that besets us. We are to shake off discouragement. Put on "the garment of praise for the spirit of heaviness," (Isaiah 61:3, KJV).

My 9-year-old son had a tournament baseball game recently. It was a hard-fought match, a single-elimination game. During one inning, our team's regular pitcher was tired, and the back-up pitcher got hit in his pitching hand at last bat. So the second back-up pitcher went in and the game took a turn for the worst. He was walking so many players that the opposing team had nearly caught up. The coach called in the pitcher and asked him to switch with the current catcher (the tired pitcher). The boy came off the mound and began to openly sob. He felt like he had thrown the game.

The coach and two assistant coaches formed a circle around him and told him what they needed him to do. Then, as the boy continued to wail, the coaches began to systematically strap the catcher's protective gear on the boy. At one point we heard him cry, "No, I can't go on. I can't do it!" just as they lowered the facemask over him. They patted him on the back and said, "We really need you to do this," as they guided him behind home plate.

What a picture this paints of the discouraged Christian! He has discarded all of his spiritual armor and sat down in a pile of dust. He might even be wailing and travailing, crying, "No, I can't go on!" But Jesus begins to strap the armor back on as He says, "I know you can do this because I am on your side." He lifts him to his feet and guides him back into the battle. "You can do all things through Me because I am strengthening you."

So friend, you might have hit on hard times, but get back into the game. The rest of us are depending on you.

The Oven Door

> Everyone should be quick to listen, slow to speak, and slow to become angry.
>
> James 1:19, NIV

I was teaching a rural home-based preschool program and had just arrived at my student Seth's home, a single-wide trailer. The goal of our program was to help parents understand how to assist their children to succeed in school. So to help fulfill that goal, our job as teachers was to encourage parents to sit with us and the students at the dining room table as we made our way through the various activities.

Seth's mother had other plans. Since she worked full-time at the factory which her husband also worked at, she had no interest in joining us. She wanted to use the whole ninety minutes to catch up on her soap operas.

As Seth and I made our way through puzzles and educational games, he wondered what the snack would be for our lesson that day. I had always brought a fun-to-make snack that I kept back until the very end of our time together as a sort of carrot to dangle, ensuring that all lessons got completed. I informed him that we would be mixing up some pretzel dough and shaping it into the letters of his name. I had already asked his mother for permission to use her oven.

When the time came to bake the pretzels, I set the timer for ten minutes while Seth and I practiced printing his name. Finally, the timer began to buzz. I slipped on the oven mitts left on the counter beside the oven and proceeded to open the door. It wouldn't budge. I gave it a few more hard tugs and then the gravity of the situation hit me. I had a choice to make: I would either have to interrupt Madam Leisure and tear her away from her soaps, *or* let the pretzel letters become crispy critters.

I gently broke the news to Seth's mother that I was in need of her services in the kitchen. She wasn't upset with me, but as she made her way to the kitchen she began to rehearse things about that "lousy husband" of hers. Apparently, she had asked him on several occasions to fix the oven door problem and her requests had gone unfulfilled.

Anyway, she was working herself up into quite a lather as she reached for the oven door handle. The vision that met my eyes seemed too incredible to believe. The adrenaline must have been pumping through her rather large frame as she gripped the oven door handle and ripped it clear off the hinges! There she stood, eyes blazing, holding the hot oven door in the middle of the kitchen. After regaining my composure, I slowly cut a wide circle around her, and pulled the golden letters of Seth's name from the now cavernous oven opening.

This event made me look more closely at the destructiveness of anger. How many times do we let that emotion get complete control of us? We yank off the oven door of our soul, self-control, the part of us meant to contain the burning heat of our anger, and throw caution to the wind. We destroy things, or even worse, relationships, and embarrass ourselves in front of others. And every time we allow anger to take charge of us, we have empowered it that much more.

Ephesians 4:31 tells us, "Get rid of all bitterness, rage and anger, brawling and slander, along with every form of malice," (NIV). God does not want us harboring these poisons in our beings. These things only bring destruction. Romans 8:6 tells us, "For to be carnally minded is death, but to be spiritually minded is life and peace," (KJV). Every single thing we get angry about in the flesh *can* be handled in the spirit of life and peace.

So the next time you get frustrated with things and people, just remember: burning pretzels is no reason for burning anger. Keep a cool head and it's just possible that you could figure out a calm way to rescue the pretzels. And you'll probably still have your oven door right where it belongs.

Jesus Talked to a Tree

> Then He said to the tree, "May no one ever eat fruit from you again." And His disciples heard Him say it.
>
> Mark 11:14, NIV

Jesus spoke to a tree. Yes, you read that correctly. Jesus actually spoke to a tree. Now let's get out of our religious mindset and look at this for what it really is. Forget that this is a story in the Bible and pretend you read this in the newspaper this morning. Jesus **talked** to a **tree!**

With this Scripture in mind, I went out in my front yard and spoke to a tree. You see, this tree has a hollow area in the trunk, and some of the upper branches have died. So I stood there and talked to my tree and spoke life to it and blessed it.

Okay, I hear you saying, *That's a little crazy.* Not any crazier than Jesus walking up to a fig tree with twelve other men and saying, "May no one ever eat fruit from you again." And He walked away.

Can you imagine the look of amazement on the faces of the twelve disciples? You know they had to be exchanging glances that said, "Okay, He's been working way too hard lately. I mean, dealing with the Pharisees, raising the dead, healing the blind, feeding the multitudes. It's all been too much for Him. He needs to take some time off, get away for a weekend. Come on. He just talked to a *tree*!"

But what they may not have realized was this: Jesus did not start this conversation. The tree did. The Scripture says, "In response . . ." Jesus was *answering* the fig tree! *Oh, no,* you groan, *this problem is even worse than I thought!* Hold on a minute. Let's unpack this. When you back up a few verses, you can see the tree was actually saying something to Jesus. As I stated in an earlier writing, the tree was saying with its leaves, *I have fruit.* But this was a deception. When Jesus came to find some fruit to eat, the truth was evident: this tree was lying. So, in response, Jesus pronounced a curse and told the tree that no one would ever eat fruit from it again.

Okay, so is this some kind of lesson on a new twist in botany? What is it Jesus was trying to convey? First of all, your words have power. Secondly, when you mix your words with your faith, your circumstances will begin to change. What is it in your life that needs to change? What circumstances are talking to you and telling you that life is bad and will never change? Or even more directly, what is Satan telling you that is contrary to the Word of God? In all of these cases, you need to be responding to the situation and speaking the changes God wants into those circumstances.

Lastly, Jesus was looking for fruit. It's time to do a little self-examination and make sure that when Jesus looks at your life, He will find something pleasing to Him. Don't let Him walk away disappointed.

The Fig Tree Died

> In the morning, as they went along, they saw the fig tree withered from the roots. Peter remembered and said to Jesus, "Rabbi, look! The fig tree you cursed has withered!"
>
> Mark 11: 20-21, NIV

The disciples were astonished when Jesus stood and talked to this tree. Now, hours later, they saw the impact His words actually had on a physical, material thing. Over a period of mere hours, this tree had actually died! Although it did not happen immediately, the point is *it did happen*.

The problem that we as believers face in our walk of faith is we give up too easily. We pray a prayer of faith, but if we don't see something happen in the next fifteen minutes, we immediately begin to entertain thoughts of *I guess it didn't happen*, or *why doesn't God answer my prayers?* or *maybe it isn't God's will*. Essentially what we have done is planted a seed and fifteen minutes later we have dug it up and said, "I guess God just isn't answering my prayer," or "This doesn't work."

When Jesus spoke to the fig tree, He had no doubt that what He had just said would come to pass. He spoke those words and knew the tree was beginning to die from that very moment. He also wasn't surprised to see hours later that the tree was completely withered.

So, here is what I have personally learned from this Scripture. When you pray a prayer, say for healing, believe that your problem is beginning to wither and die from that moment. The next day, when your symptoms persist, speak to your body. And remind yourself that this sickness or health problem is in the process of withering and dying. Take your thoughts captive and make them line up with what the Word of God says about your healing. Remember that we walk by faith, and not by sight. We are not to look at our circumstances, but look at what the Word says about our circumstances. Do not give in to fear. Take your stand of faith and watch this problem die.

Speak the Word over your situation and *expect* to see it change. Don't worry about how long you will have to stand. Just continue until you see your problem wither away.

Your Negative Situation Needs Attention

> The next day as they were leaving Bethany, Jesus was hungry. Seeing in the distance a fig tree in leaf, He went to find out if it had any fruit. When He reached it, He found nothing but leaves, because it was not the season for figs. Then He said to the tree, "May no one ever eat fruit from you again." And His disciples heard Him say it. In the morning, as they went along, they saw the tree withered from the roots.
>
> Mark 11:12-14; 20, NIV

Jesus was physically hungry and was looking for a way to solve this need. He saw a fig tree that beckoned to Him to have His need fulfilled there. It was calling for His attention to be shifted from the task at hand, namely traveling to Jerusalem, to its own deceiving temptation. What Jesus did then, in response, was to curse it. In essence, He was saying, "This stops now! This is over!"

This tree had logically been alive for several years since it had grown leaves to the point it could have produced figs. But Jesus was telling it, "You are finished!" And it was.

One Sunday morning, I was sitting in church listening with my full attention on the pastor's sermon. Suddenly, I became aware of a sore feeling on one side of my throat. There had been a diagnosis of a lump on my thyroid years before. Both the doctor and the surgeon had hurriedly pushed for me to have immediate surgery to have all or most of my thyroid removed, which would have left me on medication and a roller coaster of endocrine gland levels for the rest of my life.

Instead of having the knee-jerk reaction most people, including myself, give in to when a doctor pronounces a diagnosis, I cast down the fear Satan was trying to get me to buy into, and I did not make any immediate decision. In Philippians 4:6, Paul admonishes us, "Do not be anxious about anything, but in everything, by prayer and petition, with thanksgiving, present your requests to God. And the peace of God, which transcends all understanding, will guard your hearts and minds in Christ Jesus," (NIV). This verse leaves no exception for anything to be worried about. Not a lump, not a diagnosis, not a cancer-scare. Nothing. Absolutely nothing. Instead of fear, I began to seek God in daily prayer. Instead of doing what people in the world normally do, I wanted to know what God wanted me to do. He is my Creator after all, and He knows my future. Why would I not consult Him first? Is He the Lord of my life or not? Is He really in charge?

Getting back to the church service, this problem was voicing its need of attention in a much louder way than it had previously done. Of course, the spirit of fear was right there to seize any opportunity to push me off the course of faith. I was at first annoyed, then aware of the fear that was present, and then thoughts of *This is feeling serious. Maybe a doctor should look at this, etc.* You know the drill. I then heard the Spirit of God speaking over the annoyance, over the fear, even over the pastor's voice, "This problem is wanting attention. Give it some attention! Give it the Word!" I understood. Like the fig tree, this affliction was speaking to me, and it was high time I spoke back to it in faith. I reminded it of the fact that just four days prior, I had cursed it and it was in the process of dying. I immediately felt the pain diminish measurably.

Faith works, believer! Speak to your problems and watch the faith God has provided you do its work.

Cursing the Fig Tree

> The next day as they were leaving Bethany, Jesus was hungry. Seeing in the distance a fig tree in leaf, He went to find out if it had any fruit. When He reached it, He found nothing but leaves, because it was not the season for figs. Then He said to the tree, "May no one ever eat fruit from you again." And His disciples heard Him say it. In the morning, as they went along, they saw the tree withered from the roots.
>
> Mark 11:12-14;20, NIV

Jesus was hungry and saw a fig tree in the distance. This means He had to walk somewhere off the path He was on to check it out. This tree was, in its own way, beckoning to Him with a message, *I have something you need.* In a sense, this tree was being deceptive. I have learned fig trees normally put out leaves at the same time the figs appear. Therefore, when Jesus saw the fig tree "in leaf", it would follow that the tree should have figs on it.

How many of us Christians are doing this in our lives? How many of us profess to be Christians, to have Biblical principles at work in our lives, but yet the fruit we bear is non-existent, or at best, rotten. This tree had nothing to offer Jesus. But think about this: the fig tree had been busy. Its roots had brought up water and nourishment. The tree had spent energy in producing leaves. How many times have you been as busy as a hamster in a wheel, and had about as much to show for all your effort? Think about how much Jesus has invested in your life. What fruit does He get to reap from all His efforts?

I don't know about you, but in heaven one day, when Jesus is reviewing my life, I want to hear, "Well done, good and faithful servant." I *don't* want to hear, "Well?"

Here is another point: Not only was Jesus disappointed in this tree's lack of fruit. He actually *cursed* it. What does this mean? Simply put, to curse something means to cut off blessing from it. If you could picture people living alongside a creek or riverbank to get water for their crops and livestock, you would see an example of the blessing. If someone upstream dammed up the water so these people had no water and everything was drying up and dying, this is an example of a curse. Jesus was not blessing a fruitless tree. He cursed it and it completely withered and died.

Again, I want the Lord's blessing in my life. I don't want my hopes and dreams to dry up and die simply because I am not bearing the fruit that brings blessing to my life.

So let's take a lesson from a simple tree. Let's get busy doing the job God designed us for—bearing fruit for His Kingdom.

Caterpillar to Butterfly

> Do not conform any longer to the pattern of this world, but be transformed by the renewing of your mind.
>
> Romans 12:2, NIV

The word *transformed* in our Scripture text actually means "metamorpho" in the original Greek. This is the word we get *metamorphosis* from. Now, we have all seen pictures (or the real deal) of caterpillars spinning a cocoon, and after a period of time, emerging as a beautiful butterfly. But a few years ago, I heard the latest scientific research on the matter. The news stunned me.

Before the recent research, scientists formerly believed that various parts of the caterpillar somehow morphed into the parts of the completed butterfly. But here is what they found out: all of the material makeup of the caterpillar actually turns into a liquid material—a soup, if you will. During the process of metamorphosis, the molecules of the caterpillar completely reorganize to make a butterfly, complete with two wings, two antennae, and this time, only six legs. In other words, this creature is completely different from the former creature.

Remember the words of the Apostle Paul? "The old has gone. The new has come!" (2 Corinthians 5:17, NIV). This describes exactly what the new birth does for us. Spiritually we are completely new. Just as a butterfly has a totally different perspective now that he is flying in the air instead of plodding on the ground, so we should be looking at all things with new eyes. That is why Paul tells us in Romans 12:2, "Do not to conform any longer to the pattern of this world, but be transformed by the renewing of your mind," (NIV).

Although our spirits were born-again, our minds were not. The Bible tells us here that our minds do not have to conform any longer to the world, but can be as transformed from the old to the new as that caterpillar was to a butterfly. It's a whole new way of thinking, of choosing, of relating, of living. Just be warned: the world around you—your family, friends, neighbors, and co-workers--won't understand your new way of living anymore than a group of caterpillars looking up at a butterfly can understand his. They might talk bad about you, insult you, make fun of you, and rain on your parade.

It is only because their feet have never left the ground.

Restored

> "I will restore you to health and heal your wounds," declares the LORD.
>
> Jeremiah 30:17, NIV

Restore. I was thinking about this word. I found it in the above text and in another that reads, "I will restore the fortunes of Jacob." (see Jeremiah 30:18) I got to thinking, *What does restore mean?* Literally it means to store again. What I was getting from this little moment of contemplation? That in order for God to restore something, He had to have it in store to begin with.

In other words, in order for God to restore your health, He had to have health stored in you already. And if He had a store of health in your body at the start, then what happened to it that it had to be restored? It was stolen! By whom? The devil! John 10:10 says, "The thief comes not but for to steal, kill and destroy. I am come that they might have life and have it more abundantly," (NKJV).

The big difference this fact makes is this: when a person is in need of healing, his or her thought process usually goes something like this, *I am sick and I need God to heal me.* There is nothing sinful about this, but look at this idea: *God gave me health. Satan stole it.*

I am resisting Satan, and God is restoring my health to me. There is a definite paradigm shift from the first thought process to the other.

Think of it this way. The "I am sick" statement speaks of a victim mentality. "God, I am a victim. I need you to stand in the gap for me and do something for me." The second statement is more of an offensive stance. It says, "This is mine and no thief is going to take it away from me." Another verse of scripture says "Men do not despise a thief if he steals to satisfy his hunger when he is starving. Yet if he is caught, he must pay sevenfold, though it costs him all the wealth of his house," (Proverbs 6:30-31, NIV).

If you find the thief who stole your goods, your health, your finances, or whatever, according to scripture he will have to repay sevenfold. Don't lie down and play the victim. Get up and demand that the thief gives back what he took, plus more. It's not enough for him to simply give back what he took. No. There is a penalty involved. In our justice system, if the police found the bank robber at the scene of the crime with a bag of money in his hand, it would not be enough for the robber simply to hand over the goods to the police. There is a penalty for stealing. There is a trial, there is jail time. My point is this: instead of demanding back what is yours, you need to plunder the devil. Don't just believe for healing. Take the devil to task and make him wish he would have never started anything with you.

Look at your storehouse. Is everything where it should be? Is anything missing? Take inventory. And then take the sword of the Spirit in your hand and, by God's power and grace, get back what belongs to you. Be restored.

Parasites

> But if the Spirit of Him that raised Christ from the dead dwell in you, He that raised up Christ from the dead shall also quicken your mortal bodies by His Spirit that dwelleth in you.
>
> Romans 8:11, KJV

Being in the middle of a battle for the healing of my body, I have been paying attention to Scripture verses like the one printed above. I had phoned a ministry I support to agree with me in prayer. Previously that day I had been meditating on this very Scripture. The woman who prayed with me also quoted this verse in her prayer. Then she went on to pray, "Father, in the Name of Jesus, I curse the life force of this dysfunction. I command it to die. And I pray that you would restore life to her body."

Her prayer stunned me. She was putting forth the idea that something which had life in it was living off of my body. That sounds like a parasite. Then I recalled how Jesus had cursed the fig tree. What happened to that tree? It died. How? Jesus had effectively removed the life from it by cursing it. In other words, He prayed against the life in that tree.

What I get from this line of thought is that when something has attacked my health, it is actually living off of the life in me. For example, when you get an infection, what is it literally? It is a virus or some type of harmful bacteria that has been able to multiply in your body. What is necessary for it to multiply? It must feed on something—YOU! So, when you curse it, you are stopping the life that is enabling this parasite to continue to live in you.

Think of a curse as a river that is dammed up. The lack of water for those who live alongside this river is a lack of life. It is death. When you cut off your sickness by speaking life into your body, you have dammed up the source of life that affliction has depended on.

God told us, "I have set before you life and death, blessing and cursing. Therefore, choose life." (Deuteronomy 30:19, NKJV). When you decide to stand for life, God will back you up. Your parasites' days will be numbered.

Little Bitty Batter

> As the Philistine moved closer to attack him, David ran quickly toward the battle line to meet him. Reaching into his bag and taking out a stone, he slung it and struck the Philistine on the forehead. The stone sank into his forehead, and he fell facedown on the ground.
>
> I Samuel 17:48-49, NIV

I was sitting at the championship game of my daughter's fast-pitch softball team. Our team was up to bat and a tiny girl of about eleven years walked up to the plate. I heard a chant coming from the dugout, "Little bitty batter with a great big bat! Little bitty batter with a great big bat!"

I was thinking about what they were saying. What that chant meant was, "She may be little, but she can wallop that ball!" That got me to thinking about David. In light of the giant's intimidating size, David looked pretty much like a zero. He was young, inexperienced, and small. But he had a big faith. There was a fire burning in him that no giant could quench.

The Word tells us "no weapon formed against you shall prosper," (Isaiah 54:17, NKJV). No matter what the giant looks like, God promises the giant will not prosper if our trust is in God alone. David was not trusting in his own ability to slay Goliath. He had already declared his faith in his God. He had spoken to Goliath and told him what was going to happen to *him*. He said, "This day the LORD will hand you over to me, and I'll strike you down and cut off your head. Today I will give the carcasses of the Philistine army to the birds of the air and the beasts of the earth, and the whole world will know that there is a God in Israel," (verse 46). His faith was totally leaning upon God. God would have to hold him up.

On the flip side, when the twelve spies came back from spying out the Promised Land, ten of them were so impressed with the giants who lived in that place, that they were willing to give up the land to the giants. They saw themselves as grasshoppers compared to the giants. Proverbs 23:7 says, "As a man thinks in his heart, so is he," (NKJV). These men believed they were grasshoppers and so they were. Their courage melted away and fear prevented them from getting what was rightfully theirs.

Joshua and Caleb, on the other hand, were ready to take the land. They said that through trusting God it was theirs for the taking. And forty years later, when the doubters had all died out, Joshua and Caleb were finally allowed to get their inheritance in the Promised Land.

So it's okay that you may be a "little bitty batter". Just as long as you remember that you carry "great big bat". Don't worry. God will help you swing it.

What Do You Think?

As a man thinketh in his heart, so is he.

Proverbs 23:7, KJV

* * * * * * *

God has given us tremendous power in our thought life. This Scripture actually tells us that what we think about, we will become. And because of the natural downward trend of our sinful nature, the outcome usually is not good.

For example, do you think of yourself as defeated? Then you will generally walk in defeat. Of course, you might accidentally stumble into a victory now and then. Even a blind squirrel comes up with an acorn once in a while. Your life, for the most part, will flow in the direction of defeat.

Do you think of yourself as poor? Maybe not living in a cardboard box poor, but do you always feel as though you just barely get by? If there is any bump in the road will you be destroyed? Your bank account testifies that this is your lifestyle. The reason is that is how you think in your heart.

Do you feel condemned by God? If you are a born-again Christian, this is a deception in your mind, because Paul tells us in the Word, "There is therefore now no condemnation to them who are in

Christ Jesus," (Romans 8:1, NKJV). But if you think of yourself as condemned every time you mess up, you will live a life of condemnation.

If you find yourself in the above descriptions or any variation of them, what are you to do? This is how you think and this is your experience. There is a way out. Romans 12:2 tells us, "Do not be conformed any longer to the pattern of this world, but be transformed by the renewing of your mind," (NIV). When you renew your mind to God's Word, your pattern of thinking will change. If you feel defeated, begin meditating on the verses such as these: "We are more than conquerors through Him (Christ Jesus) Who loved us," (Romans 8:37), "I can do all things through Christ Who strengthens me," (Philippians 4:13, NKJV), "No weapon that is formed against you shall prosper," (Isaiah 54:17, NKJV). If you see yourself as poor or lacking, instruct your mind in the Word, "My God will supply all your need according to His riches in glory by Christ Jesus," (Philippians 4:19, NKJV). If you feel condemned, begin to search the Scriptures for verses that tell you who you are in Jesus.

Once we have switched allegiances, from darkness to light, we do not have to live anymore under the curse of this world. All of those negative perceptions of yourself are from the Devil who desires to have you under his foot, when in reality *he* is under *your* foot. Of course, if you have strayed from the path of godliness, you need to repent. And do not wait another minute. The longer you procrastinate, the more advantage the Devil has over you. Once you have placed yourself back under God's protection, keep your mind on the things of God. You will operate in more victory and joy than you ever thought possible.

He Holds Victory in Store

He holds victory in store for the upright.

Proverbs 2:7, NIV

* * * * * * *

I cannot describe to you the mix of joy and incredulity that I experienced when I first meditated on the truth of this Scripture. Since I consider myself to be in the company of the upright, I knew this promise applied to me. The verse is very short, but within this little line is a huge revelation. If we take it apart and see what it really contains, we will have more to process than we could ever conceive.

He Who is *He*? Since all the books in the world cannot begin to explain Him, let me just remind you of a few of His attributes. He is God, the Almighty One. He has the ability to do *anything*. There is nothing in the realm of possibility He cannot do that is in line with His character. Jesus said, "What is impossible with men is possible with God." He is the Creator of everything that is seen and unseen. He is beyond time, and distance is nothing to Him. In the book of Psalms, it is declared "darkness is as light to You," (Psalm 139:12, NIV). Nothing is beyond His sight—He sees all.

Holds When God holds something in His hand, Jesus says, no one can snatch it out. No one has ever been able to wrest anything out of God's hand. He wins every wrestling match He is determined to win.

Victory Webster's Dictionary describes victory as "a decisive winning of a battle or war."

Store Have you ever walked into a huge warehouse? Were you amazed at the amount of stuff that can be stored and stacked up to the rafters? In the book of Job, a description is given of the magnitude and power of God as it tells of the storehouses where God keeps hail, snow, and even bolts of lightning! Have you or your kids ever tried to preserve a snowball or hailstone in the freezer? What happens to it over time? It changes its consistency and then finally disappears. But God can store these items---and lightning! This is impossible in human terms. I believe God is showing us here that He is in total control of *everything!* And He has a warehouse full to the rafters of *victory!* Every victory you will ever need in your life is there.

I once heard a story about a faithful believer who had tried his best in life to please God. But he struggled through the whole journey to feel successful as a Christian. He wondered why other Christians seemed to enjoy victories in their lives that always seemed to elude him. Why did God seem to favor them over him? He didn't want to complain, but this did seem a bit unfair. Then the day came that this believer went home to be with the Lord. Humbly, he asked the Lord about this concern. The Lord said, "Come with Me." He followed Him to a storehouse. Upon entering, he was amazed at an abundance of beautifully wrapped packages of all shapes and sizes. "What are these, Lord?" he asked. "These are all the provisions I had for victory in your life," replied the Lord. "But you never asked Me for them."

I think this scenario is common among believers. But it is tragic when we consider what our mission is. We are to bring light to a dark world for Christ. God knows we will have need of provision to accomplish this objective. Every soldier in the military is issued what he will need to succeed in his mission. Will God do less? It is a tragedy we are not putting a demand on God for what we need to fulfill His will. If we do not have what we need for the task, then the task is not getting done. And people will perish eternally because of it.

Jesus is "a very present help" (Psalm 46:1, KJV). Charles Spurgeon has this to say about the subject, "Covenant blessings are not meant to be only looked at; they are intended to be appropriated. Even our Lord Jesus is given to us for our present use. Believer, do you make use of Christ as you should?" (Morning & Evening, p. 261).

Upright The upright are those in right standing with God, those who have exchanged their righteousness for the righteousness of Jesus. Make sure you are one of the upright. It won't do you any good to beg God for His blessings when you are not one of His.

So read the Word and see what God has put in His storehouse for you. You will be amazed.

Camouflage

> Then the man and his wife heard the sound of the LORD God as He was walking in the garden in the cool of the day, and they hid from the Lord God among the trees of the garden.
>
> Genesis 3:8, NIV

* * * * * * *

My husband, Karl, and I were attending a weekend seminar at our church. We had left our children—Lesli, Ariel, and Jesse—at home. Friday night went well as far as our kids were concerned, but Saturday was a different story. We had told our kids that they needed to clean their rooms and do homework before they watched a movie. During a break, my husband decided to call the kids and see how things were progressing. My oldest daughter told my husband that Jesse, my youngest child, had not cleaned up anything in the house. When Jesse overheard Lesli's end of the conversation, he became livid. Because of his outburst, my husband warned Jesse that he would be coming home immediately to mete out punishment.

What happened next should be a very familiar scene for all of us if we just think about it. Jesse went into his room to devise a plan. He dressed in his camouflage coveralls and slipped out of the house through his window. He then ran out into the woods, hoping not to be detected, as my husband came down the driveway. In the process of running from his punishment he fell and scraped his face on a rock. A few minutes later, he decided that instead of running, he wanted to be reconciled to his dad. He was tearful as he told his father how sorry he was.

The reason this scenario should seem familiar is that this is a fleshly reaction to sin. When we sin, our first reaction in the flesh is to hide. Even though we know that our Heavenly Father knows our sin, in our flesh we are deceived into thinking we can hide it from Him. When we've run far enough and stumbled and fallen and hurt ourselves, though, we realize that running and hiding is not what we really want. What we truly desire is to be reconciled to our Father. So we come out of hiding and run into His arms.

What kind of camouflage are you sporting these days? Are you ignoring the promptings of the Holy Spirit? Are you justifying it to a friend so that you can feel better about yourself? Do you attend a church that winks at sin, and this gives you the idea that God does too? Are you self-medicating so that your conscience is deadened to the reality of the destruction you have welcomed into your life?

It's time to come out of the woods and take off the camo. It's time to do the things that will make your life usable to God. It's time to get real.

Ephesians 5 & You

> But among you there must not be even a hint of sexual immorality, or of any kind of impurity, or of greed, because these are improper for God's holy people. Nor should there be obscenity, foolish talk or coarse joking, which are out of place, but rather thanksgiving.
>
> Ephesians 5:3-4, NIV

A few days ago a situation involving Christians and crude humor came to my attention. In order to address the situation adequately from Scripture, I turned to Ephesians 5:1-5 (NIV). Let's take a look at that verse by verse.

Be imitators of God, therefore, as dearly loved children. (v. 1) First of all, Paul calls us to imitate God. Not to be cliché, but you have to ask yourself, *what would Jesus do?* We really need to ask ourselves, *Could I really see Jesus doing that?* When you are tempted to go along with the crowd and laugh at some dirty joke, try to see God in your mind's eye and make the decision He would.

Secondly, he said that we are to imitate God *as dearly loved children.* We are to imitate God the way a child imitates his father. A child who respects his father wants only to honor him by his behavior, especially since he knows he is dearly loved by his father. Have you ever watched a little boy imitate his father? He might flex his biceps, checking to see if his muscle looks anything like his dad's. Or he might want to hammer in a nail just like Dad.

Next, in verse 2, Paul says we are to "live a life of love, just as Christ loved us and gave Himself up for us as a fragrant offering and sacrifice to God." When we live a life of love, we put off a beautiful fragrance to everyone around us, but especially to God.

So far, he has told us what *to* do. Now, he tells us what *not* to do. Here he tells us in verse 3: "But among you there must not be even a hint of sexual immorality, or of any kind of impurity, or of greed, because these are improper for God's holy people. Nor should there be obscenity, foolish talk or coarse joking, which are out place, but rather thanksgiving. For of this you can be sure: No immoral, impure or greedy person—such a man is an idolater—has any inheritance in the kingdom of Christ and of God." (NIV).

Wow! Paul tells us to stay away from these obvious acts of the flesh. He knows that the Devil will use these devices to keep us from our inheritance in the kingdom. These sins will trip us up and keep us from bearing fruit for God. God wants us to experience His blessing in our lives. Ephesians 5 tells us how.

Building on the Rock

> He that dwelleth in the secret place of the Most High, shall abide under the shadow of the Almighty.
>
> Psalm 91:1, KJV

The topic of our discussion today is on the importance of establishing a growing relationship with God. Not only will your life be carried to new levels of understanding and joy, but God will afford you protection that is not made available to the world.

Jesus talked about this when He taught the disciples a story involving two men. These two men were in the process of constructing homes, or dwelling places, if you will. In this story, the houses represented the course of their lives. Jesus said the first man built his house on sand. Now, most of you reading this for the first time who have any inkling of how to build a decent house, know this is, for all intents and purposes, a really stupid idea. But, like any stupid idea, it does have its advantages. For one thing, building on sand is *easier*. Walls can be put up without doing all that tiresome digging. Do you realize how much work it is to dig all the way down to solid rock and then dig that out for the bottom floor living area of the entire house? It's huge!

Another benefit is that building on sand is *faster*. Skipping the digging part means that walls and roof go up extremely quickly. You can be moved in and having your house warming party, while the neighbor who is building on rock is just getting his footings built.

Let's put this in perspective. You are the man building on rock. In other words, in life, you are not just grabbing every opportunity life affords you. You are seeking God, reading His Word, attending church and Bible studies. You are putting in the time to know God, receive from God, to understand His ways and His character, endure trials, watch the power of prayer, and suffer persecution. Your roots are going deep, even though your plant above the surface does not have much to show for. You are busy sacrificing time, resources, and opportunities. You are giving of yourself.

Your neighbor, the one building on sand, on the other hand, seems to be living the good life. Things seem to be going well for him. He has plenty of time to enjoy the pleasant things of life and plenty of fun-loving friends to enjoy it with. You look at him and ask, "God, why does this worldly person seem to have a much better life than me? He seems to worry about nothing and has all the pleasure anyone could ask for. Why am I going through all this trouble and sacrifice?"

God sees all and the Scripture says God knows this person's day is coming. The storm is coming and he is unprepared. He will meet with destruction and none of his fun-loving friends will be found. You, on the other hand, will have a life that will be able to withstand the blast of the storm. When all the dust settles, your life will still be intact and you will maintain peace in your heart.

I'm reminded of the fairy tale of the three little pigs. We have the same principle here. The three were sent out to seek their fortunes. They all built houses within the vicinity of each other. All had the same goal and the same opportunities to fulfill them. But the first built his house with straw. It was easy and inexpensive. The second built his house with sticks. Again, it was easy and inexpensive. The third, however, built his house with bricks. Much more expensive. Much more time-consuming. In some versions, the first two pigs were lying in the lap of leisure while their brick-laying brother was still laboring away.

But the storm came. The wolf huffed and puffed at each house to see which would give way. In the less pleasant accounts of this story, the piglets did not run to the brick house of piglet #3. No, the wolf blew down their houses and gobbled them up. When the wolf came to the third house, not only did he fail to blow it down, but his obsession with having another pork dinner brought about his final demise.

So take the time to build on a rock. You won't regret it.

Speak to Your Mountain

> "Have faith in God," Jesus answered, "I tell you the truth, if anyone says to this mountain, 'Go, throw yourself into the sea,' and does not doubt in his heart but believes that what he says will happen, it will be done for him. Therefore I tell you, whatever you ask for in prayer, believe that you have received it, and it will be yours."
>
> Mark 11:23-24, NIV

Have you ever really considered what Jesus was telling us in this Scripture? Let's look at this part, "Say to this mountain . . ." Stop right there. Jesus told you to speak to your mountain. For just a minute, think about how you pray. When your back is against the wall, when there is some crisis you are unable to resolve on your own, how does your praying sound? Does it go something like this? "O Lord, You see the problem, You know the mess I'm in. Do something, Lord. I don't know what to do. Help!"

Jesus instructed us to speak to our mountain. The mountain represents whatever problem we are facing in our lives. Instead of speaking to God about our problems, Jesus is telling us to speak to our problems about God.

Just prior to this conversation with his disciples, Jesus had cursed a fig tree on His was into Jerusalem. Several hours later, on the way back out of the city, the twelve saw the fig tree Jesus had cursed and it was withered from the roots up. They were astonished and asked Him about it. He then spoke to them the words from our text above. The essence of what He told them was this—speak directly to the problem! He said if you believed, if you had faith, whatever you asked for would be done.

One day, when I was meditating on this verse, this line of thought occurred to me: Jesus picked the biggest object possible that the disciples could see in nature, a mountain. He was emphasizing that there is no problem too big for your faith in God to tackle.

Here's a thought: we have all seen natural disasters reported on the news. How many times have you seen the damage a tornado has done? Tornadoes have picked up cars, roofs, even entire buildings! But how many times has it been reported that a tornado picked up a mountain? Even the extreme magnitude of the force of a tornado has never picked up a mountain and moved it.

But your faith can.

Picture yourself standing in your yard with a bowling ball sitting on the grass in front of you. This bowling ball represents a relatively small problem in your life. If Jesus had told you to speak to your bowling ball, that your mustard seed-sized faith is sufficient to move your bowling ball and cast it into the sea, could you believe that? But He didn't limit the power of your faith based on the Word of God to a bowling ball-sized problem. He only limited its power to the biggest problem you could imagine. A mountain is no match for the Word of God.

Get out there and speak to your mountain. Then get ready to see your problem move out of the way.

Just Ducky

The mind controlled by the Spirit is life and peace.

Romans 8:6, NIV

It had been a hot summer with a dry spell thrown in for good measure. One neighbor's pond had completely dried up. So after a few good heavy rains, the pond was looking good again. Walking one morning, I noticed that the wild ducks had come back. I wasn't sure what they were doing exactly. They just seemed to be aimlessly paddling about. Maybe they were just enjoying what they liked best.

This scene got me pondering the nature of ducks. God made them to be drawn to water, to live near water, to get their sustenance from water. God gave ducks a special relationship with water. They don't have to consciously think about getting in the water. It's just something they do.

This reminds me of the nature of God's children. When we are born again, God gives us a new nature, the nature of our recreated spirits. God made us to be drawn to Him, to live near Him, to get our sustenance from Him. We don't have to consciously think about getting into God's presence. It's just something we do.

If this is the case, then why do we find it so hard to pull ourselves away from all the distractions we are surrounded by? Our spirits are drawn to Him, but our unrenewed minds are not. When our souls (which are comprised of the mind, will, and emotions) have not been continually exposed to the Word of God, then these parts of our being will fight against our relationship with God. Throw in a sick, tired, or lazy body, and you've got a recipe for a minimal relationship with God at best.

Romans 12:2, says, "Do not conform any longer to the pattern of this world, but be transformed by the renewing of your mind. Then you will be able to test and approve what God's will is-- His good, pleasing and perfect will," (NIV). According to this Scripture, you will know what God's will is. His specific will for your life is what is on His heart. And when you begin to tap into what is in God's heart, you have a great basis for a deep relationship with Him.

When your mind is renewed, your will has to be conformed to His. And when God has your mind and will in line with Him, your emotions are soon to follow. Then your mind, will, and emotions simply pick up your body by the nape of the neck and it will fall right into step.

Practically speaking, when your soul and body are following the leading of your born-again spirit, you will have no problem taking yourself into the presence of God every day to worship Him and seek His face.

It will be as natural to you as a duck takes to water. Then your life will be just ducky.

The GPS Mess

> Do not conform any longer to the pattern of this world, but be transformed by the renewing of your mind. Then you will be able to test and approve what God's will is, His good, pleasing, and perfect will.
>
> Romans 12:2, NIV

I recently read the story of a woman who had a GPS installed. She had no idea how to program it for specific destinations, so any time she needed directions, her husband had to help her out. On this particular outing, she had to travel fifty miles on the interstate to get to the next turn-off. She had just settled in to this part of the drive when, to her surprise, the lilting woman's voice with the British accent announced to her that she needed to prepare to get off the interstate at the next exit! Knowing full well that she needed at least fifty more miles under her belt, she rebelled against the voice coming from her dashboard. Every two miles this "voice" was more adamant than the last time, and needless to say, the driver was very much annoyed by the time she actually got to her exit. (She didn't know how to silence the voice.) When she got home and talked with her husband, she realized that he had put in the wrong town name.

This incident got me considering a certain spiritual aspect of our lives. We are driving down the road of what we know is obedience to God or God's will for us, really planning on nothing more than going from Point A to Point B. We have our GPS (God Positioning System) in our hearts. Then a thought comes to us unexpectedly that we don't need to proceed this way anymore. This comes from outside of our hearts—the dashboard. This is the SPS (Satan Positioning System). Depending on how confident we are as to whether or not we are on the right road determines what we do next. Some people will panic, thinking that they never did know anything for sure about God. Others will hesitate and pull off to the shoulder and sit there listening to the voice while they have spread out the map and completely double-checked or triple-checked everything, including the car's engine! Others, completely confident in the direction God has shown them, quickly silence the voice and don't even slow down.

Now, for those who don't slow down, the thought, the "voice" from the dashboard, may attempt to redirect them. But this will probably only endure a few times, each attempt being weaker than the previous, until finally it fades out all together. For those sitting on the shoulder, the voice is much stronger and louder, nearly screaming at them to take the nearest exit. And for those who panicked in the first place, the voice has soothed them into a state of false calm.

Just what am I driving at here? Only that when you are on the path that God has for you, Satan will be the "misprogrammed" GPS, trying to get your life as far away from God's plan as possible. His words will seem so right and true that they may throw you for a loop.

The only way to discern what you should do is to know in the first place Who is directing your path and stick to the directions (the Word of God). Then your GPS won't leave you in a mess.

Squirrely Thieves

> Catch for us the little foxes, the little foxes that ruin the vineyards.
>
> Song of Solomon 2:15, NIV

Last summer I went out to our small grove of fruit trees to check on the abundance of small pears ripening on the branches. The previous two summers my daughters and I had learned the art of canning one red wagon-load after another of the bumper crop. Sixty-two quarts each summer to be exact. It looked like this year would be no exception. The pears still needed two more months to ripen, but I wanted to be ready.

A few weeks later I went to check on the trees and thought I was seeing things: not a pear was to be found—not within reach, not on the very top, not even a rotten one on the ground! Who had done this? The most likely answer was a bunch of squirrels.

I called the agricultural extension office. My guess was confirmed. The gentleman I talked to said squirrels are most likely to be fruit thieves in a year of drought. He informed me that squirrels had actually taken tomatoes out of his garden and the produce could be seen fifteen to twenty feet up in the branches of nearby trees!

He told me that other than taking up squirrel hunting, I really didn't have any options.

This experience provoked my thinking: who are the squirrels in your life (and mine, too)? I'm not referring to those colorful characters in your life which tend to annoy you. What I am referring to are those distractions, temptations, and idols (anything that means more to you than God) that are stealing the spiritual fruit from the tree of your life. What thieves are keeping you from reaching the lost, serving the Body of Christ, praying for the sick, providing for those in need, teaching your children the Bible, and spending time alone with God? Are your squirrels named Hobbies, After-School Activities, Having Coffee with Friends, Sports, Making Money, Facebook, etc? You know what I'm talking about.

Now, none of those things in and of themselves are wrong, but even too much of a good thing is not a good thing, and therefore can become sin. We've all heard it said, "You've got to keep the Main Thing the Main Thing." When the Main Thing in our lives gets so crowded out by the Minor Things, then the Main Thing is no longer the Main Thing.

I would like to point out a deceptive thing about squirrels. Simply put, they are cute! Just to look at a little squirrel scampering around the yard gives you a good feeling! But when you've had your whole crop stolen by the little critters, you begin to take a closer look. In reality they are rats (rodents) with bushy tails. They can be destructive. They are thieves. And suddenly, they are not so cute.

Just like the "squirrels" in our lives. They may seem harmless and they make us feel good, even productive. But the little thieves deceive us and we don't even realize that the whole time we are enjoying the experience with them that they are stealing us blind! And it doesn't take long for our spiritual lives to begin to drift backwards. Before we know it, our lives are indistinguishable from the world. We live our lives in the same ways. Actually, what the world sees when they see our lives looks about like my fruit trees did last summer—no fruit. Well, there is one exception. Rotten fruit. *That* is what we have to offer the world.

In Matthew 12:33, Jesus gave us no middle ground. He stated, "Make a tree good and its fruit will be good, or make a tree bad and its fruit will be bad, for a tree is recognized by its fruit," (NIV). In reality, we don't have a choice of whether or not we will bear fruit. The only choice we get to make is if we are producing good fruit or bad fruit. Maybe we need to face the facts and go squirrel hunting. We might need to cut back on some activity or eliminate something altogether that is stealing too much of our time away from God's purpose for our lives. The author of Hebrews said it this way, "Therefore we also, since we are surrounded by so great a cloud of witnesses, let us lay aside every weight, and the sin which so easily ensnares us, and let us run with endurance the race that is set before us," (Hebrews 12:1-3, NKJV). We need to evaluate what is holding us back from being kingdom builders and lay those things aside. We need to hunt it down. And keep it from stealing our fruit.

Well, I've just checked on this year's pear prospects—and they look mighty promising. Excuse me, please. I've got some squirrels to hunt.

Prodigals & Pigs

> Do not give dogs what is sacred; do not throw your pearls to pigs. If you do, they may trample them under their feet, and then turn and tear you to pieces.
>
> Matthew 7:6, NIV

Have you ever experienced a broken relationship and were unsure of whether or not God was leading you to reconcile with the person or to avoid the relationship altogether because of the person's toxic character?

About a week ago I woke up with the following going through my mind. I saw a revelation about discerning and having wisdom in certain relationship situations. The two situations in the Bible that I am about to discuss seem to have inconsistent conclusions on how to handle difficult people in our lives.

The first one is the story of the prodigal son. In this story, as you may recall, a young man with an older brother, decided that he did not want to wait for his inheritance until his father's death. He wanted it now! And the implication here is this: "Father, I wish you were dead so that I could have my inheritance immediately." So, the father gave the son what he craved. The young man then proceeded to go off to a distant land where he blew the money on whatever suited his fancy—parties, drinking, and the like. When his money was gone, so were his friends. Then a famine hit the land and this young rebel was in desperate need. He found a job feeding pigs (a most humiliating job in light of the fact that pigs are unclean to Jews). He finally hit bottom and decided to go home and ask for his father's forgiveness. He was even willing to be treated as a hired hand. The father would not hear of such a notion. He quickly reinstated his son and then threw a big party for him, much to the chagrin of his older brother.

The second situation is the advice Jesus gives about bad relationships. Matthew 7:6 says, "Do not give dogs what is sacred; do not throw your pearls to pigs. If you do, they may trample them under their feet, and then turn and tear you to pieces," (NIV).

This appears to mean that there are certain relationships that need to be avoided simply because they invite abuse. How does this dovetail with the prodigal son story which shows that one should forgive and reconcile?

Here is what I believe the difference is: character. When Jesus talked about "dogs" and "pigs", He of course, was not talking about the literal animals, but the character qualities they represent. Dogs were not viewed as the loyal pets our society loves. They were despised as nuisances. Pigs, as stated earlier, were considered unclean to the Jews.

I believe Jesus was saying that when you are in a conflict with someone who consistently exhibits bad character, you are wise to avoid them, because they are bent on your destruction. Paul even says, "Evil communications corrupt good manners," (I Corinthians 15:33, KJV). And Jesus said, "Be wise as serpents and innocent as doves," (Matthew 10:16, ESV).

In the story of the prodigal, this young man gave into the dual temptations of greed and rebellion. He acted out and then realized how unwise he had been. He repented and asked forgiveness of his father. This action signified the fact that his character was still intact, though badly bruised. His repentance, or change of heart, showed his true nature, which had hit a bump in the road, so to speak, but was still there. A dog or a pig, though has a consistent nature, that if encountered in a confrontational manner, will always be destructive.

We are not to give dogs what is sacred. So just what is sacred? The truths pertaining to God. Do not throw your pearls to pigs. And what are pearls? Things in life that carry great value.

The point? We need to be discerning when it comes to these difficult situations in life. Yes, God wants us to be loving, but He also wants us to be wise.

A Farmer Went Out to Sow

A farmer went out to sow his seed.

Mark 4:3, NIV

Maybe you are thinking, *what's the spiritual impact of this verse on my life?* Well, let me tell you, it's huge. God has just been peeling back layer after layer for me about this fact and that's why I have to write about it. It is just bubbling over in my heart.

The above verse comes from a time when Jesus was teaching His disciples. He was introducing a parable which would teach His disciples the ways of the kingdom of God. Later, Jesus would even state that this parable was the key to all the others. In verse 13 He says, "Don't you understand this parable? How then will you understand any parable?" So this is pretty doggone big.

So what is a seed? The Christian Student Dictionary states, "The part of a flowering plant that can grow into a new plant. A seed contains food to get the new plant started and information so that the seed can grow into just one particular kind of plant."

So a seed is little container of reproductive material. It is able to reproduce itself completely. In the plant world, the seed is able to copy itself usually in multiples. If you plant one corn seed, you don't just get one corn seed back. According to the Iowa Corn Promotion Board and Growers Association, one ear of corn can produce anywhere from 500-1200 kernels of corn. That is powerful!

According to our definition above, this seed is even more incredible when you consider the fact that each one contains food to get the new plant started and information to tell the plant how to grow. The nourishment and the blueprints are all right there. Everything that is needed for success has been packed into that little package. Don't tell *me* there wasn't a Master Designer!

So who is the farmer? I think there are a couple of good answers. The first answer is the farmer is God. The Bible says in Habakkuk 2:14, "For the earth will be filled with the knowledge of the glory of the LORD, as the waters cover the sea," (NIV). God is all about getting His message everywhere. In the time period in which Jesus spoke this parable, farmers did not have the massive, complicated machinery to get their crops into the ground like they do today. They had bags of seed strapped onto them. They would reach in, grab a handful of seed, and swing it in a half-circle to broadcast it to the waiting soil. God is in the business of broadcasting His Good News even today.

Another answer which is not mutually exclusive of the preceding one is the farmer symbolizes each of us believers. God said, "Let Us make man in Our image," (Genesis 1:26, NKJV). If God is the sower, and He made man in His image, it stands to reason that God would expect us to be sowers as well.

What seed are we supposed to be sowing? What does the seed represent? In verse 14, Jesus blatantly states, "The farmer sows the Word." God is busy sowing the Word in the soil of our hearts.

And after it comes up in our lives, we are to be planting it into the lives of others and expecting a bountiful harvest.

So, strap on your bag of seed, grab a handful, and let it fly! Then get ready for an abundant harvest!

The Dirty Window

> If there be any virtue, or if there be any praise, think on these things.
>
> Philippians 4:8, KJV

The other day, as I was driving down the road, I noticed a car coming up behind me. The entire car was completely covered in dust. As I looked up again a few minutes later, I noticed a different car behind me. It, too, was covered in dust, exactly like the first one. Then I noticed yet a third vehicle coming up behind this one. You guessed it—it was covered in dust. It was then that my lightning-fast mind realized what was going on—I was looking through my own dirty back window. When I looked through that window, everything looked dirty, regardless of its true condition.

This experience led me to think of my attitude. How many times has a rocky start to a day colored the entire remainder of the day, regardless of how it truly played out? How many times has my first quick judgment of someone, either by what they did or said (and my possible misinterpretation) lead me to look through that same "window" every time I met them without checking to see the condition of my own soul to see if perhaps a cleansing of my attitude were in order?

In James 1, we are told to be quick to listen, slow to speak, and slow to become angry, (see verse 19). I believe James is admonishing us here to slow down and give a person or a circumstance a chance to be properly evaluated before we jump to conclusions. If we leap in haste, as the old saying goes, we can repent at leisure.

I remember hearing the story of the man coming home on the subway after a hard day's work and all he wanted to do was relax for his commute home. But his hopes were soon dashed as realized he was sharing a car with a man and several out-of-control children. He couldn't believe it—the kids were running and shouting, and many of the other commuters looked as though they were shocked at this scene as well. The incredible thing was that everyone was disturbed--except for the father. He just sat there oblivious to the entire spectacle.

After exchanging glances with fellow commuters, the working man knew what he had to do—confront this man about his apathetic attitude toward his children. So he asked the man why he didn't correct his wayward children. The man looked up at the speaker as if he had just snapped out of a trance.

He responded, "I'm sorry if my children have troubled you. We have just left the hospital where my wife died."

Can you spot the dirty window here? All of the commuters in that car were all looking through the same dirty pane, but the truth of the matter did not come clear until someone sought out the facts. Once the surface was clean, everything looked completely different. I'm sure everyone in the car that day who were so incensed at the behavior of these children, were quickly moved to compassion when they realized what these kids had just been through. Somehow their rough-housing didn't seem to be a problem anymore.

We all fall short in this area. We all do this. But the sad thing is, in most of our situations, we look at the circumstantial evidence and assume that our conclusions have to be right. Many times we don't ask questions past our assumptions and we believe we have the facts straight. Or we let something bad that has happened to us color our whole day with a sad grey shade of discouragement.

But the Bible gives us numerous admonitions to do just the opposite. We are told by the apostle Paul to think on what is true, noble, just, pure, lovely, and of good report, (see Philippians 4:8). He wasn't telling us to just think happy thoughts. He was telling us to focus on these things in direct contrast to what our circumstances might be. He was saying, in essence, that no matter what life has thrown on the window of your soul, clean it off with the washing of the water of the Word. Focus on the good things in your life that your Heavenly Father has provided.

And when you look through that clean window, you'll probably see Him smiling back at you.

Believing God

"Have faith in God," Jesus answered.

> Mark 11:22, NIV

Are you believing God today? Now, I'm not asking if you believe *in* God. I'm saying *are you believing God?* What has God told you that He would do for you that is just too much for you to conceive? In the book of Ephesians, God promised to do exceedingly, abundantly above all we can ask or think. (See Ephesians 3:20.) So forget trying to understand it. Paul tells us in I Corinthians 2:9-10, "No eye has seen, no ear has heard, no mind has conceived what God has prepared for those who love Him—but God has revealed it to us by His Spirit," (NIV).

What that passage tells us is that there is no way our finite minds can contain what God has for us. We just can't understand it. But it can be *revealed to us by the Holy Spirit.* Okay, God has made a way for us to get this. So what's the problem? Why can't we believe God?

Well, a big part of believing God is the ability to hear God. Merely reading the Bible is not the same as hearing God speak to you through His Word. I heard the true story of a man who had a booth at a carnival. He asked people to ask him for any chapter and verse in the entire Bible and he could quote it. He had memorized the *entire* Bible. But it meant nothing to him. He was as lost as a goose in a hailstorm.

Romans 10:17 says, "Faith comes by hearing, and hearing by the Word of God," (NKJV). When the Holy Spirit reveals to our hearts a truth from God's Word, this is when faith comes.

You might say, "I was reading the Bible the other day, and God showed me something and I had faith to believe it. I prayed, but nothing happened. It must not be God's will for me."

My response to that is this: seeing a promise in the Bible for the first time and expecting something to happen is like planting a seed in the ground and an hour later digging it up to see if you have gotten a flower. "It must not be God's will for me to have a flower," you might say. Or you might be working out with weights at the gym for the first time. After twenty minutes of huffing and puffing you check your floppy biceps and say, "It must not be God's will for me to have strong muscles."

Having faith and believing God *takes time.* I've heard it said that a faith not tested is a faith not trusted. We often don't really know the depth of our faith until God takes us to the very bottom of it. When we empty ourselves of all that we hold dear and just hang onto God with everything we've got, we come out of that trial quite different than when we went into it. As John the Baptist said, Jesus must increase, we must decrease. (See John 3:30.) Again, this process takes time. But that is when the Bible comes alive in our hearts and we begin to glorify God and tell others about Him. And, believe me, this is time well spent.

Worthless Pursuits

"Thou shalt have no other gods before Me."

Exodus 20:3, KJV

* * * * * * *

One enemy of prayer is what I call "useless pursuits." People get involved in all kinds of activities and all their spare time is squandered away. These activities do not even have to be immoral to be an all-out enemy of prayer. As a matter of fact, these pastimes are usually neutral in nature. They could be out of balance as far as time is concerned. Here is an example: shopping. Now you men out there are breathing a huge sigh of relief. But don't relax too much. I will set my sites on you in a moment.

I must confess I am not a shopper, but I realize that most women simply love to shop. Several years ago, when my first baby was born, I quit my job to stay home with her. I happened to run into a neighbor down the street and told her of my career change. She got all excited and talked about how we could do things together because she stayed home, too. She chatted on and on about how she simply loved to shop, and how we could go together sometime. I gently informed her that I was not a shopper because I would see things at the mall that I didn't know I needed. And I also didn't have a budget for that. I let her know that I was open to other ways we could make plans to get together. She never contacted me again. How sad. She also had numerous yard sales in the summer time. I understood why.

Let me explain something here. I know that we all have to go shopping at times because we all need things. What I am driving at is the amount of time that we spend doing it and the reasoning behind it. The Bible says in Colossians 3:23 (NIV) "Whatever you do, work at it with all your heart, as working for the Lord, not for men," (NIV). I Corinthians 10:31 declares, "Whatever you do, do it all for the glory of God," (NIV).

I believe the litmus test in these circumstances is "Does this activity bring glory to God?" If you need clothes for yourself and your family, then shopping qualifies as ministry to them and brings glory to God. But if you are so obsessed with your image and how you look that your time is spent in pursuit of these ends, you are an idolater.

Jesus said, "For where your heart is, there your treasure will be also." (See Luke 12:34). He also stated that you cannot serve two masters: God and Mammom. Mammon is referring to the world's system of operation. Have you bought into the ideas of the world? Do you derive your sense of worth and value from what the world tells you or from what the Bible tells you? Is God your treasure or is shopping what brings you fulfillment?

Okay, now on to the men. What about golf? What about organized sports? How much time do you spend in this activity on a weekly basis? A better question is this: what do you spend more time pursuing: your relationship with God or keeping up with the latest sports statistics?

You see, if the lion's share of your time is spent doing these things, you aren't truly glorifying God. You might just have a worthless pursuit on your hands.

Courageous Sheep

> For He is our God and we are the people of His pasture . . .
>
> Psalm 95:7, NIV

Anything you read about sheep will usually talk about how timid and easily spooked they are. They are defenseless, having no horns or sharp teeth. They are suspicious and shy. But I have noticed something in recent weeks that has me looking at sheep a little differently. You see, we have six sheep of our own. Several months ago we acquired a Border Collie puppy we named Lexi. We have fallen short in our attempts at training her not to chase the sheep unless we need her to corral them.

Sometimes when Lexi has managed to crawl under the gate to the pasture, she relentlessly chases these sheep into a corner of the pasture and bites at their wool, pulling out small chunks of it. Then she begins to chase them again. Although the sheep are disturbed by this unruly behavior, I have noticed a sense of courage in these animals. They seem to sense that this "predator" isn't something of which to be terrified. They have learned that, if they will just hold her off from her little tirade long enough, they will soon be relieved of their tormentor. They have watched us time and again chase this little nuisance all around the pasture and drag her off with the aid of a leash. The sheep know that their trial will soon be over and peace and quiet will soon be restored.

I couldn't help but see the parallel in my own life. The Bible calls us "sheep" on several occasions and I know that all those descriptions of sheep I listed earlier apply to me. When the storms of life rage over my life, or when the enemy of my soul attacks me, immediately my heart begins to panic. I don't feel equal to the challenge and I feel that my adversary should have no trouble defeating me. But then I remember that my God is in control. If I trust Him for the outcome, I will never be disappointed. As I stand my ground against the enemy, God will make the Devil flee from me. I have nothing to fear. I have the Father Who loves me, I have Jesus interceding for me, and I have the Holy Spirit to guide me. If God is for me, who can be against me?

So, when Satan has my back up against a wall and there seems to be no way out, I need only to remember that, by His grace, when I am weak, then I am strong.

What have I to fear? I am His sheep. He is my Shepherd.

With Him at my side I can be a courageous sheep.

Freedom

> Where the Spirit of the Lord is, there is freedom.
>
> 2 Corinthians 3:1, NIV

In church a few weeks back, the praise team sang a song with the verse "where the spirit of the Lord is, there is freedom." I pondered the word *freedom*. Doesn't everything really come down to freedom? Aren't all of our laws centered on the topic of freedom? They are all about what freedom one person has as opposed to another. Church denominations have been built around what belief system a certain group of people are free to believe. Parents have the job of deciding what freedoms their children will be allowed to have and which will be restricted from them.

God has given each human being a free will. He created Adam and Eve and told them what His will was for the tending of the garden and for obeying Him. He didn't create them to be robots with no choice in the matter of the Tree of the Knowledge of Good and Evil. He gave them the freedom to disobey Him and in so doing gave them the freedom to love Him as well.

So what does the concept of freedom have to do with our relationship to God? After all, Paul said that he was a bondslave of Christ. Let me explain how the two harmonize. God made every person a worshipper and therefore a slave. "What?" you might be wondering, "I thought you said God gave us a free will? How can we be slaves?" Well, God made us worshippers. Every person will worship someone or something. And you will be a slave to whatever you worship. If you worship a person, i.e. following after a celebrity or being in a codependent relationship with someone else, you are a slave to that person. You might not have a problem with worshipping a person, but material items might be your "god". Things like money, food, vacations, position, sports, a business, or other things might have your attention. You give these things all your time, attention, focus, and energy. You will even make important sacrifices, including relationships, in order to advance your ambitions regarding this "god". Therefore you are a slave to this person or thing. This "god" commands your time and choices. You are a slave.

That being said, God, in His benevolence, has given us the choice whom or what we will worship and serve. When we worship and serve Him, we are now free to be who He created us to be. When we worship ourselves, others, and things, we find ourselves in bondage and thus our true selves are squelched under the weight of our oppressor. When we worship Jesus, we are free to enjoy all that He provided us in His death on the Cross. We are free to be healthy, to be righteous, to have access in prayer to the Father, to have the help and wisdom of the Holy Spirit, to be provided for, to be protected, to be forgiven, to have mercy and grace, to have eternal security.

On the other hand, if you choose to reject the worship and service to God, you are free to be deceived, to be in bondage, to be under the curse of the law, to live in anxiety and depression, to be in doubt, to have Satan oppressing you at every turn.

So the choice is up to you—how will you use your freedom?

Fruitless Trees

> Neither can you bear fruit unless you remain in Me.
>
> John 15:4, NIV

Our apple trees didn't bear any fruit this summer. The man at the agricultural extension office told me it was because we had too much rain in the spring. The bees simply couldn't get out to pollinate the blossoms.

Pear trees must be a different story apparently, because we had branches breaking with the abundance of fruit. I thought about this yesterday when I went out to collect the last pears on the tree. I had visited those pear trees many times in the past few weeks to gather in little red wagonloads of pears and to plan what to do with so many. I prepared my canning supplies and bought more jars. But the few visits I had made to the apple trees were disappointing to say the least. There was no planning going on in my thoughts there. All I had were higher hopes for next year.

I wonder if this is how God feels about us and how we live our lives. How many times in the Scriptures are we reminded to bear much fruit, to have the fruit of repentance, etc.? Does God feel disappointment as He stands before our fruitless branches? Does

He sigh when He thinks about our potential, but then walks away with an empty wagon?

On the contrary, when we are fruitful, is God delighted to think about all He can do with our lives that are moving in sync with His will and purposes for us? Does He envision the sweetness that others will experience as a result of the good fruit we have born in service to Him?

God has given us the bees to pollinate and produce fruit, namely the Holy Spirit. It is now up to us to allow the Holy Spirit to do what only He can do in our lives, and in the lives of those around us.

Apple pie, anyone?

What's That Smell?

> Get rid of all bitterness, rage, anger, harsh words, and slander, as well as all types of evil behavior.
>
> Ephesians 4:31, NLT

* * * * * * *

I stepped out into the fresh spring day to take my teenage daughter to her tutorial. The first thing that hit me when I ventured outdoors was the scent of skunk. A guilty-looking dog quickly moved out of my way. Hoping for a change of aromas when I entered my van, I was unpleasantly surprised. The fragrance of skunk actually smelled better than what met me in there! I hadn't driven the van for a few days and now I remembered that the last time I had used it, I had detected a slightly mysterious smell. Now it was more than that. It was a force to be reckoned with. Added to that, we had to pick up the boy who carpooled with us in just a few minutes. My daughter and I hurriedly investigated the interior to see if we could uncover the source of the odor. The two of us found a few pieces of trash, but could not find the culprit. We did our best to air out the van before we arrived at the neighbor's house.

Later on that day, while waiting at my daughter's music lesson, I had need of a napkin, so I reached in the pouch on the backside of the passenger seat. My fingers landed on a plastic baggie.

I pulled it out and realized that I had found the source of the repulsive problem. Apparently, my ten-year-old son had stashed the leftovers of a snack into the pocket directly in front of his seat. What I held in my hand was a glop of disintegrating mystery food. A tiny whiff of the funky substance was overwhelmingly awful. The search was over.

Have you ever sensed something not quite right in your life? It may be hard to put your finger on, but you know it's there. It may be an ugly attitude you have toward a certain person who just rubs you the wrong way. It might be something that's chipping away at your peace, like anxiety, dread, or fear. It might even be a little root of bitterness. Or maybe it's just something that seems out of sync. At any rate, it leaves an odor in your life that just isn't pleasant.

"Well," you tell yourself, "It's not a big deal. Actually, it's probably nothing."

Take it from me. The longer the "smell" stays in your life, the stronger the aroma. Very soon, it will smell like something died in there. At that point, others will be able to detect the odor in your life. They will begin to react to it and the result will not be pleasant. It's time to conduct an investigation. Just like my van situation, you must begin to examine the dark places of your heart. You must reach your hand in where you don't want to go and examine what you find. When you find it, it will not be rocket science to figure out what to do with it. You must get rid of it at once! There is no reason to hang on to a bad attitude or a negative emotion. Nothing can justify keeping your baggie of rotten stuff. It has to go!

Paul admonished us to "Get rid of all bitterness, rage, anger, harsh words, and slander, as well as all evil behavior" (Ephesians

4:31, NLT). Paul knew that these negative emotions are not only sin, but they continue to spread within our very beings. Like a cancer, these adverse forces will spread until they have consumed everything we are.

So dig deep and get ruthless with sin. You will notice that life is starting to smell rosy again.

Receiving Jesus as Your Savior

Choosing to receive Jesus Christ as your Lord and Savior is the most important decision you will ever make!

God's Word promises that "Everyone who calls upon the Name of the Lord will be saved," (Romans 10:13, NIV). By His grace, God has already done everything to provide salvation. Your part is to simply believe and receive. God loves you no matter who you are, or what you have done. God loves you so much that He sent Jesus, His one and only Son, that "whoever believes in Him shall not perish but have eternal life," (John 3:16, NIV). Jesus laid down His life for us so that we could have Him in our lives now and forever in eternity.

If you would like to receive Jesus into your life, pray the following prayer out loud and mean it from your heart:

Heavenly Father, I come to You admitting that I am a sinner. I choose to turn away from sin, and I ask You to cleanse me from all the effects of sin. I believe that Your Son, Jesus died on the Cross to take away my sins. I believe that He rose from the dead so that I might be forgiven of my sins and made righteous through faith in Him. I call upon the Name of Jesus Christ and confess Him to be the Savior and Lord of my life. Jesus, I choose to follow You and ask that You would fill me with the power of the Holy Spirit. I declare that I am a child of God. I am free from sin and full of the righteousness of God. I am saved in Jesus' Name. Amen.

About the Author

Cherie Hammers has taught and written material for Bible studies for over ten years. Her passion for the Word of God, desire to learn more, and being surrounded by beautiful countryside has inspired her to help others through the lessons God has taught her. Cherie lives with her husband, their three children, and a menagerie of farm animals near Nashville, Tennessee.